NOT JUSTICE
BUT MERCY

NOT JUSTICE
BUT MERCY

Kelly Turner
with
Cliff Dudley

New Leaf Press
P.O. BOX 311, GREEN FOREST, AR 72638

First Edition
1988

Many names and places have been changed to protect the innocent. It is not my intent to harm anyone, but to simply tell my story.

Library of Congress Catalog Number: 87-82615

ISBN: 0-89221-148-2

Contents

DEDICATION

To my mother who prayed and believed
that God would change me
and
To Rev. Coy Barker who helped make the
change possible.

Kelly's mother, Kathleen

FOREWORD

Here is a book that can change the destiny of lives. This is a real life story of tragedy and triumph. It is written in terms this generation understands and relates to in today's world. Early in Kelly Turner's life he felt pain that very few people feel.

I was with Kelly when it was dark and his future looked hopeless. God gloriously changed his life in one of our services. Immediately, I knew God had His hand on his life.

For an inspiring, refreshing, faith-building and life-changing experience, I encourage you to read this book. You will weep with him, and you will also shout and rejoice with him.

I am confident that if you will take a long, sincere, and profound look at this life changed by faith in the Lord Jesus Christ, you will experience the same saving and changing power in your own life.

I have experienced firsthand the testimony written in this book, and I am so glad that Rev. Turner has put it into print. I have seen this testimony change lives — on television and in person. Here, truly, is a word of hope for modern man. May God bless you and yours as you read this book.

Pastor Coy Barker

Rev. Coy and Donna Barker

1

UNTIL THAT WHIPPING

"I am what?" shouted the woman. "Doctor, do you realize that I am a woman who is forty-two years old? I certainly don't need any more kids! Are you positive that I am pregnant?"

"Mrs. Turner, I am positive and if I am not mistaken, you are not only going to have one but two! It's a good thing that you have those two older daughters to help you out. You are going to need all of the help you can get!" the doctor said grinning.

"Thank God my husband is retiring from the military. I couldn't handle two more kids all over the countryside at my age, or any age as far as that goes. Doctor John, are you certain...real certain?" she longingly asked again.

"You certainly are welcome to get a second opinion, Mrs. Turner, but I am certain that you will get the same answer if you go to a hundred doctors...Yes, you are pregnant! You and your husband should be very happy at the prospect of having twins."

"Sure," the woman thought. "I can't keep him home now."

Several months passed and the doctor's diagnosis was correct. A boy and a girl were born into the Turner household. The girl was named Kim and the boy (that was me), Kelly.

Soon after we were born, my dad retired from the military, and the family moved to a small town in Alabama called Benton. Benton was almost midway between Selma and Montgomery on famous Highway 80. My folks bought a house almost on the highway. Little did they know that in a couple of years, we would all have a ringside seat to one of the most famous marches of all time. Yes, The Freedom March would pass a hundred yards from our house.

Benton was a quaint, civil war era town of about twenty families. Most of the residents were descendants of aristocrats of Civil War days. An old mansion, now restored, was brought down by some "blue leg raiders" during the war.

Part of the original family had always lived there.

Old man Ryan came later from South Carolina in 1901 to Benton on a motorcycle and started a little farm with a hoe.

He ended up being a very wealthy man. He and his descendants then pretty much owned the town, as they were the ones with all the money.

So if you weren't fourth or fifth generation in Benton, you were a newcomer. We lived there for over ten years and were still considered outsiders.

My folks were really having trouble, but in those days and in that town nobody divorced. If it did happen, it wasn't talked about. Divorce was something to be ashamed of. My father was never home so my mother tried to cover it up as much as she could. Kim and I didn't know what was going on, but I am certain that Judy and Betsy, my older sisters, knew something was wrong. I didn't realize the anguish, heartache and pain my mother was going through, because of my father's running around and never coming home. I guess it was compounded by living in a small town that was like Peyton Place.

In Benton everybody knew everything about everybody. We probably were looked on rather shadily, but I didn't know that at the time. But Mom knew and of course, appearances were important to her. There were black sharecroppers who were almost slaves. They were totally dependent. We were poor, but we had a black maid named Perline. How I enjoyed sitting on her fat lap! Perline never sat at the table with us. She would get to our house at the crack of dawn and have breakfast ready for us when we got up. I was always up before anyone else. One day I was sitting on her lap, and she was feeding me by taking a bite of grits and then giving me a bite. She'd take a bite and I'd take a bite. Perline didn't have any teeth and probably hadn't had a bath, because the shack she lived in didn't have running water. We paid her by letting her do her wash at our house once a week and giving her leftover food. I think we probably added four or five dollars a week in cash to poor Perline. But everybody in Benton had a maid and a cook, even the poor people and we were pretty poor.

Suddenly, my mother came into the kitchen and saw me eating after this old black woman. I was told to get down. I knew Mama was mad, but I didn't know why. When Perline was out of sight, Mama grabbed me by the neck and said, "Kelly, you listen and listen good. Don't you ever let me see you eating after Perline. White folks don't do such things. You hear me? Just so you don't forget, I'm going to whip your bottom.''

Did I ever get a licking! That day I knew the "difference" between white folks and "niggers". Most of my friends were black, and until that whipping, I didn't know the difference even though it was right in the middle sixties when all of the civil and racial unrest was going on (especially in Alabama). We would hear talk about the blacks wanting to ride on the front of the bus and share our toilets and things like that.

"Next thing you know," one man said, "Those niggers will want to be going to school with our kids. Thank God the government doesn't have any say about church or we would have them wanting to pray and sing with us. That Rev. King, from Atlanta, is stirring up blacks all over America. Heard the other day there's going to be a march from Selma to Montgomery. If they're not careful, the highway will be full of dead niggers."

The march took place all right. Martin Luther King led thousands of blacks on a freedom march. The march from Selma to Montgomery was part of his "passive resistance" program encouraging non-violent demonstrations, for which King received the Nobel Peace Prize.

Judy yelled, "Here they come! There are miles and miles of them."

I didn't understand what was going on, but I stood on the hood of the car and watched in awe. There was screaming, yelling, and rock-throwing, but nothing was going to stop them then. That was a day of reckoning for us whites. New laws were passed and blacks would have their rights because of that march which went by my house.

The first year I went to school was the year the federal government passed integration laws that allowed blacks to go to school with whites. So my parents, along with almost every other white family in the county, formed a private school.

They refused to let us go to school with blacks.

The irony of it all was that I went to church every week; I got medals, pins, certificates, and Bibles for perfect church and Sunday School attendance year in and year out. Everyone considered themselves devout Christians. One of our deacons would stand at the back door until all the "faithful" came in and then lock the doors so no one else could get in. His reason was every now and then a black would wander in and sit down. He would make them leave saying, "Niggers can't come to church with white people. Now we know that you're a Christian, and we know that you have to have church too, but the nigger church is down there." He would point down the road and send them on their way.

One time the women's club from church found out that Billy Graham was coming to Montgomery. So my mother asked, "Why don't we get a couple of carloads of people and all go see and hear Billy Graham!"

One of the ladies in the church replied, "Oh we don't want to go see him; I hear that he lets blacks come to his crusades."

That was the kind of racial unrest and prejudiced mentality which was in the South in those days. I didn't understand it and it was a "run-of-the-mill, everyday thing." I started first grade in the private school. My older sister, Judy, was in high school, and Betsy was going into sixth grade. My mother put us in school and my father paid our tuition. When I started school, I realized for the first time that fathers should be at home with their families.

There was only one main road coming off the highway

into town. Often, I'd be walking back from the store with a moonpie and a Coke — dirty, barefooted, wearing nothing but shorts. I would see Dad's car turn onto the road and would I get excited! I remember one car that he had custom ordered.

It was a big Plymouth Fury III with salmon-colored paint and a white top. Was it sharp! I don't know why I'd get so excited. He had never been around that much and never showed me any love or paid attention to me. Dad was forty-four when I was born and just seemed to have lost all interest in his family. He had developed a pattern of staying out to one or two o'clock in the morning after going to the club with the guys. One thing led to another. He went into business for himself, and instead of staying out late at night, he started staying away days at a time. Dad opened a tavern in a little, old "honkytonk" town called Brownsville about seventy miles away. He would go over there and be gone days at a time. So when I would see his car coming into town, it would excite me. I would wave him down and jump into the car with him. Alabama was hot in the summer, and when I would jump in with Dad, it seemed like it was freezing because of the air conditioner. I'd ride to the house with him, and then I'd follow him wherever he went.

Usually when Dad was home, he and my mother would fight.

Mom would yell, "Where have you been?"

"Don't worry about it; I've got a business to run!" he'd snap.

I would tug on his shirt-tail, trying to develop some kind of communication. I wanted him to stop and talk to me or spend time with me or something...anything! I needed a dad.

However, he'd take care of business and leave. He'd leave the tuition, lunch, and the grocery money, pick up his mail, and be gone.

I would stand in the driveway and wave bye, and my dad never even looked in the rear view mirror as far as I know. I never got consciously angry at him over it. I didn't understand it. I didn't think that my dad was leaving because of me, but I couldn't understand why he wouldn't spend time with me. I never understood why I wasn't important to him. I didn't ever think about my sister's or mother's feelings.

Perhaps the reason was I was the only boy. I had friends and their dads were always around. They came home at four or five in the afternoon after work, and they would go hunting, fishing or play ball. The first time I really realized that everybody noticed I didn't have a dad was when Dave Lions, a teenager in the church, asked my mom, "Do you think Kelly would like to go out with me and my girlfriend and shoot guns?"

That was one of the most exciting things that had ever happened to me. Some guy wanted to take me out and do something with me. I went with them on a Sunday afternoon and shot 22 rifles. I realized during the time we were out that this guy felt sorry for me because my dad was not doing this with me. He took me on as a little brother. I realized for the first time my dad wasn't doing for me what other dads did for their kids.

All the time Mom tried to keep his "goings-on" secret.

One night I looked out the window and saw a bunch of lights flashing everywhere. It was just starting to get dark. My dad was coming home from the tavern he owned drunk and cut the corner too short and drove the car in the ditch. Mom had to call a tow truck to pull him out. Of course that was big business in Benton. That was the biggest excitement that town had seen since the "King March" which embarrassed my mom beyond words. She would hardly go around anybody for weeks, because she was so humiliated. Dad often came home drunk, but this was the first time Mother knew that everybody else knew it. He was out there cussing and hollering and "raising Sam Hill." It was like the 4th of July because nothing ever happened in that town. Poor Mom had lost her cover.

Edmond Pettus Bridge
This was the starting point of the famous Freedom March led by Martin Luther King, Jr.

2

THE AFFAIR

Dad was successful in doing civilian contracts on military bases. Craig Air Force Base was right outside Selma. It was about fifteen miles from our house. Dad did most of his contracting there while running the motor pool and doing the grounds maintenance and janitorial work. A lot of the services done on the military bases were contracted out to civilian contractors. He was so successful at Craig he started to diversify and went also to Maxwell Air Force Base in Montgomery. There, he hired a secretary. I'll call her Jane. What my dad ever saw in this woman I'll never know. In my memories, she was ugly although I wouldn't know her today if I saw her. Sometimes, if I was lucky, I worked with my dad. I would beg him to take me to where he worked. He would spend time in the office, and I would run around all over the place. He had six black guys who would cook and serve for him in the chow hall on the military base.

Jane was the Gal-Friday type, doing the book-keeping, accounting and acting as Dad's secretary. As a kid I didn't know they had anything going, but they did. For a couple of years I spent time around her, and I must say she was "real nice" to me. My mother had probably known of the affair for a long time. I suppose out of self-preservation she finally told us that Dad was seeing another woman. It really didn't shock me. Of course, I really didn't know what "affair" meant.

One night Dad came home "drunker than a skunk." He cried around but wouldn't say, "I love you," or "I care about you," but wanted to give money as a token of love. He said all sorts of things that he wouldn't say when he was sober and smelled like this other woman's perfume. She had probably kicked him out because of a fight or something. It was only seven o'clock at night, and he informed us he was going to spend the night.

I don't know if we all knew a cootie was body lice, but we'd say everything of Dad's had Jane's cooties on it because he'd been with this woman, Jane.

I picked up the kitchen tongs Mom used to get eggs out of boiling water and went over to the table, really as a joke, picked up his cigarette lighter with those tongs and said, "This lighter has got Jane's cooties on it!" as I ran around the kitchen. That really cut him for he realized that I knew what was happening: He was out fooling around.

The situation intensified! You could have cut the air with a knife. Suddenly, on impulse, I threw the lighter out the front door screaming, "That takes care of the cooties! That takes care of the cooties!"

The two girls added to the insults shouting that

Kelly and Kim age 3

Jane's cooties were on Dad's shirt and his glasses. We were hurt and we wanted him to know it, in a playful way. We tormented him screeching and screaming like buzzards picking the flesh off a freshly-killed prey. What we didn't realize was that this prey wasn't dead.

Like a wounded, tormented animal, Dad's endurance ended, and he struck out with a fury like a bolt of lightning from a summer storm.

The whole family turned on him because we knew he was shacking up with Jane. He was trapped and he knew it.

He started screaming and crying in his drunken stupor.

However, then instead of drunk he seemed possessed.

He ran through the kitchen breaking everything in sight.

Then it wasn't funny. He jerked and lunged toward the TV knocking it to the floor. He grabbed the tongs cursing me as he kicked the front door open. The tongs went flying through the air and Dad after them.

He ran to his car, and we heard squealing tires as he blasted out of the driveway. We had been coming at him from every side. He had probably come home thinking he was going to make amends. As he left, I guess he felt that he didn't have a girlfriend, and he didn't have a family.

From that day on, my life was a downhill run. A few weeks later Mother said, "I'm putting an end to this!"

Of course Mom had confronted Dad many times about having an affair, and he always shouted at her, "I am not having an affair. Don't be so stupid!"

Our car was broken, and Mom didn't even have a way to get back and forth to work trying to support us four kids. By then Dad was not even buying groceries. She got her brother, my Uncle Charlie, to take her to Montgomery to an apartment where she knew this Jane lived. She instructed my uncle, "Stay in the car; I'm going in here."

Mom knocked at the door, and this Jane came to the door completely nude. Mom looked across the room, and there was my dad lying in the bed. They were caught red-handed. This woman snatched my mother into the room and started beating her. She knocked her down on the floor, sat on top of her, grabbed her by the hair, and started beating Mom's head on the floor. Mom screamed, calling my father, "Turner, Turner, help, she's killing me! Get her off!"

After this woman had beaten Mother half senseless, Dad lying there not doing anything, finally got up and pulled her off Mom. My father turned to my mother with eyes red with rage and screamed, "I've never hit you, but if you don't get out of here, I'll kill you."

Mom, in fear of her life, left. My mother came home all beaten up. She was crying and hysterical. We begged until she told us what had happened.

An hour or so later my dad walked in the house all scratched up. We assumed that his woman had got mad at him, attacked and scratched him all up and then kicked him out. He again went on a tirade. We stood our ground and he soon left.

My mother went to a lawyer to file for a divorce. The lawyer advised her, "Don't file for a divorce because he'll cut you off and not pay anything except meager child support."

So she never divorced him.

Soon after that time, he bought a house trailer and moved to Montgomery. We still lived in Benton, which was thirty-five miles east of Montgomery. My mother continued to work trying to feed us. We were poor! Dad paid a little bit of grocery money. Every now and then he'd get mad at Mom, and he would cut off the grocery money attempting to hurt her. Of course it hurt the whole family. However, he always did pay our tuition for private school. He didn't come back to the house very often after that.

Bitterness, hatred, and revenge suddenly filled my eight-year-old mind. I vowed I would get "that woman" if it was the last thing I ever did. I vowed to myself, "I'll get her one day." I planned to kill her. Of course I was eight years old so I couldn't do it. My dad fooled around because he wanted to fool around. If it had not been her, it would have been somebody else, but to me she wrecked our family. After that I'd still go to my father's work place every now and then, and she'd be there and treat me the same as she always did, which was always nice. I hated her, and I would avoid her. Eventually she put it together and realized I knew what had happened. Then she started avoiding me. I didn't know if I was going to shoot her, but I had a very vindictive and hateful spirit. She had destroyed my family and she was going to pay.

My sisters and I never talked about it. I never talked to anybody about it and I never cried. I never really sat down and concentrated on my situation, but hate was then part of my life. I knew what was happening, but I thought it was just normal. I was not ashamed of it, nor did I try to hide the hate.

The affair had wrecked not only our family, but hers as well. Her son must have suffered as much as we did.

Finally, Jane decided to quit working for my dad and for awhile she was out of our lives.

Ten years later that woman came back with a new husband and started working for Dad again! This time, however, she had married a preacher! When I found out he was married to this whore, it was all I could do every time I saw him not to tell him what had happened years ago. Until several years ago it was all that I could do not to call her husband and say, "I want to tell you what kind of a home-wrecker you married."

I could have destroyed her family, ruined, and wrecked her life and she would have gone to her grave a broken person. If I had called him and he'd said, "Well you're a liar," I could have said, "If you think I'm a liar, you call her son and ask him because her son feels the same way I do about it."

We continued going to Lowneds Academy, as no black people could go there. Hainville, the public school, had been integrated by the government. We were "Christians" so we wouldn't go to school with blacks. I remember my first grade teacher, Miss Mary Francis; my second grade teacher, Miss Sarah Cooper; and my third grade teacher, Miss Alice Lions very vividly. I never did well in school. I mean from first grade I never made the grades. My sister Kim made straight A's. I don't know if she didn't comprehend what was happening at home or if it just didn't affect her as adversely as it did me. I was tested and my IQ was as high as it should have been. I could have done the work, but for some reason I didn't want to or was distracted or whatever; I was simply not motivated. I barely struggled by from first grade all the way through school.

I had a friend named Kim Kirk. Kim and her older brother, Doug, lived at home with their mom and dad. If

I had a role model of a dad at all, I saw it in Kim and Doug's dad. He used to take us out shooting with BB guns and different things like that. Still I had never really put it together in my mind that I was that much different from anybody else.

Abnormal was normal to me because that was all I had ever known.

One time, when my sister Judy was in the twelfth grade, and she was going to bring a friend home to spend the night. My mother, even after all this agony we had been through, wanted to keep up appearances for us kids. For this one night she wanted my dad to be home for Judy's sake. She knew the club where he was. She took me down there and told me he was in the stag bar. Women weren't allowed back there. I walked down the hall into the stag bar and got my dad. He didn't have any choice but to come out because here was this little kid who had come in after him. He was furious; I mean furious! "Why'd you call me out here? I had a good hand!"

Mom said, "Look, Judy's bringing a friend home from school. Please come home and act like we have a decent home just one night for your daughter's sake."

"Take these kids and go home. I'll be home in a minute," he yelled as he went back into the club.

Of course he never came home, and it embarrassed my older sister. Supper-time came around and...no dad, bedtime came around, no dad. "Where's your dad?" was asked time and time again.

"Well he's a...a...a...," was the type of thing we had to respond with, and it soon began to take its toll on the family.

3

STARTING TO UNDERSTAND

During the summer of 1969, Dad bought us a house in Montgomery. Compared to Benton, Montgomery was as big as New York City.

I was nine going into the fourth grade. That was a great transition in my young life. I had never been in a public school, let alone with all kinds of blacks.

Public school was one "downhill road" after another.

First Kim and I were separated into different classrooms. We had never been separated. I was real close to Kim because I felt a protectiveness for her.

After the first day of school in Montgomery, I came home and said, "Mom, there were niggers there today in school."

I couldn't believe my eyes. I had never seen black kids in school with white people before. At the time, I guess I kind of thought black people didn't have souls. That was what some of the Christians taught.

One black lady was allowed to come to our church. She was a nurse of a lady confined in a wheelchair. She brought the lady in the wheelchair, put her on the pew, folded up the chair, and went to sit on the back pew. We were told blacks were "sub-human" and weren't to be treated like people.

Even little kids didn't call older black people ma'am or sir.

We called them by their first name or would say, "Hey you!" or whatever we wanted to say.

The Old South in the late sixties was almost like the slave days. But I got over that quickly! We were no longer sheltered in the private school. I didn't realize how deeply my school had affected me. (You remember everything from the time you are four or five, but once you turn eleven you start understanding.)

In fourth, fifth, and sixth grades I really started understanding what had happened: that I didn't have a dad and that it wasn't the norm not to have a dad.

I started getting in trouble at school and the office would send notes home and sometimes I'd get sent home. There were behavior problems: talking, talking, talking, "Kelly, be quiet!"

Five minutes later I'd totally forgotten about it. Possibly I was trying to get attention. I was always the class clown.

I didn't get in a lot of fights, but I was always talking. I think that more than trying to get attention from the teacher by getting in trouble, I was always trying to maintain a conversation with someone around me. This was really a pattern-setting time.

During these years my dad continued living in the house trailer doing his own thing. Sometimes I would see him on a weekend. My folks did not even attempt to live together anymore. He didn't come around, so they didn't fight. They were not divorced, only separated.

If I spent the weekend with him, I'd go to the military

Shiloh Baptist Church,
the black church

The church Kelly grew up in,
Benton Methodist Church

base with him where he did civilian contracting. I'd spend time with the people who worked for him. I'd spend time around the work site, cutting grass, or doing little odd jobs. Then we'd go home at night. He would drink a couple of beers and go immediately to bed. I'd stay up and watch TV till twelve o'clock. We never spent any time together and hardly ever said a word to each other. This situation was a real parallel of when I was a little kid in my other neighborhood. I'd see my dad drive down the street. I would drop what I was doing and run to the house as fast as I could get there. My mom and dad would fight; he'd leave money and then he was gone. He didn't even seem to know I existed. It was never, "How's school going? How are sports?" or "What's going on in your life? What can I help you with?" or "Do you want to go to a ball game?" or anything!

One time my sister and her boy friend were going to take me to a pro wrestling match. We got there and sat down. I looked across the other side of the ring toward the ringside seats and there sat my dad with Jane. He was out with her on a date. I didn't say a word, but I told my sister that I wanted to leave. I was almost in tears. They thought I was sick, so we left. I was then fully aware of what a relationship was.

He didn't belong to that woman and they shouldn't have been together. I never confronted him about it. I just blocked it out of my mind. It didn't affect our relationship because we didn't have one anyway.

Dad would come around, but we didn't spend time together; we didn't go places together; we didn't do things together.

When I would get my report card, he would come there and I would get a bawling out and that was about it.

In the seventh grade I started getting a grown-up mentality. I understood that my dad had shafted me, cheated me, and that I'd been short-changed. My mother had to work her tail off. My family had suffered embarrassment and poverty while he had a "live-it-up" lifestyle. He always drove a new car, and we always had our cars pinned together with coat hangers and clothes pins. My sister went to work trying to bring home some money. I wore raggedy clothes and pants that were too short. I didn't even get angry consciously, but rebellion started to grow inside of me. I began talking back to him. I would think, "Why in the world should he tell me something when he lives like he does? He was never there when I needed him! Never there when I was growing up! Never there when I needed help with my homework! So why was he jumping on me about bad grades? Why was he disciplining me and why was he grounding me? Why was he there then when he was never there when I needed him?"

That caused rebellion in me toward my teachers and church.

Mother took us to church every week, but I finally told her, "I don't want to go anymore."

She forced me to go another year. Finally, I quit church altogether. I was raised Methodist. I always believed in God and I always believed in satan. I knew there was a heaven and a hell. Basically, I was just a good, moral person. I always said my prayers. I never, ever from the time that I was hardly old enough to talk, went to sleep without saying my prayers. I would go through my ritual prayer, "God bless my mother, bless my father, (I even prayed for my father) bless my sisters, bless their husbands and their kids. Keep us safe, Amen."

I really thought if anybody was going to Heaven, I was. I thought I had at least a fifty-fifty chance.

When I hit junior high school, I started having the opportunity to be around guys who had dope. My concept about cigarettes, drinking and drugs was this: I had seen my dad do it, so I wouldn't do the stuff. I grew up in a little country town where, as far as I knew, there were no drugs. Montgomery was like New York City to me with drugs and alcohol. Man, there was no way that I would smoke a cigarette or a joint.

When I thought about a joint of marijuana, it was like those old school films where the guy smokes a joint, goes crazy, and jumps out the tenth story window. I thought that if you touched dope you'd go crazy.

That concept immediately began to change, and I started getting used to the darkness. In this big, metropolitan public school there were a lot of drugs. I became worldly-wise. It didn't bother me because it was so gradual. It began to look cool. The guys involved in the drugs were the most popular and the coolest. I thought, "Man those are the guys that I'd like to hang around with and be part of their popular crowd."

The cooler they were, the hipper they were, and the more access they had to drugs. So I began to hang around with those guys. When they talked drugs, I acted like I knew what they were talking about. Then it happened! I was given two joints.

4

STONED

A kid rode his bicycle over to my house. We weren't even good friends, but he gave me two joints and left. Man, I kept those things for three or four weeks. I didn't even know what to do with them. I didn't even smoke cigarettes at that time.

When I tried to smoke cigarettes, I would get so sick, I'd turn green and throw up. I was the ripe "old age" of thirteen.

One night I decided to smoke one of my joints. It was like nine o'clock at night. I went out behind a tree, way down in the middle of our back yard, where my mother still lives, and I lit it up. I didn't really know how to smoke it. I stood there and hit on it a few times. I smoked about half of it and I didn't even get a slight buzz. I thought, "There's no big deal to this."

So I threw the other half of the joint away. I had the other joint and ended up giving it to somebody else. That experience, however, took the fear and stigmatism off dope. I thought, "Why, there's no big deal to this."

Those were "famous" last words. There was this girl I

liked. I mean she was built for a ninth grader, but how built is a ninth grader? To me she was a goddess. She came from a broken home. We really related and had a kindred spirit. She didn't have a father, and her mother was a resident apartment manager of some apartments that weren't too far down the road from where I lived. I'd walk down there at night, and we would sit around and talk. At that time I had not even kissed a girl. I was pretty innocent but everybody didn't know that.

They all thought I was cool and hip. This girl really moved in the fast lane and didn't know that I had never really got high. She asked me if I smoked dope and I simply said, "Yes."

She had stolen some dope from her mother's glove compartment. Her mother smoked dope and was high all the time. She rolled two big, fat joints. I mean they were cigars! They were clean; no seeds in them, pure grass.

Probably the stuff I smoked before was some home-grown Mexican stuff out of somebody's back yard. We walked out behind the apartments to this place called Marshall's Pond. I used to ride bicycles and fish back there. It was hidden by the woods about a quarter of a mile back. We sat down beside the pond, and she got a joint and gave me one. We started smoking this grass and before long, I don't know if it was five minutes or an hour, but I was wasted. I was totally stoned. and I had only smoked about a fourth of a joint. Then this girl started getting ideas. She looked at me and said, "Come on, Kelly, let's take off our clothes."

I started getting real paranoid. I mean, I was smashed to the max. I started getting these mental pictures, like the old horror movies with this boy and girl making out in the woods when all of a sudden they're hacked up by some escapee from a crazy house. Then I started thinking, " This girl wants us to strip. Man, this has been my ulterior motive all the time." I'd been seeing her for a month and being really nice to her all for this big moment. That had been my whole goal!

I had never been with a girl, but I was smart enough to know that I wanted to. This dope was really affecting her and turning her on. I started thinking, "What would it look like tomorrow morning if my mom opened the newspaper and there was a picture of this girl and me cut up in the woods?"

I thought about this girl and me out there making out in those woods with some crazy escapee...man was I buzzing! That was my first experience of getting high, and she must have thought that I was crazy. I started screaming, "We've got to get out of here, we've got to get out of here! Let's go, come on, come on!"

"What's wrong?" she asked.

"Nothing!" I said. "Come on, we've got to go!"

I was really paranoid and tripping. I had to get out of those woods. She kept asking, "What's wrong with you?"

I kept saying, "Nothing!"

Then I got up and we headed back toward the apartments. We finally got to the parking lot, and it was like total relief.

I looked at my watch. (It was a school night. I was thirteen and it's quarter to nine.) I had sneaked out of my bedroom window. I was supposed to be back there doing homework, and I had been gone for an hour and a half. So I took off walking for home. It was about a half of a mile straight down from her apartment down this main road to my house.

I walked out of her apartment complex and got on the road going toward home. I just left her. I was walking

This was Mary Harrisons' Grocery. We called it Sug's. As a little kid I stole a lot of watermelons from there. I think Mary knew it all the time.

Benton Post Office. Size 10' X 10'

and I was thinking, "God, I'm so high; I've never felt like this before!"

I was really freaking out on this marijuana. I was saying this to God, "God, if You'll let me come down, I'll never smoke dope again."

I thought I'd never come down. "I promise, God, I'll never...just let me come down."

The next thing I knew I had passed my street, and I was a mile on the other side of my neighborhood and still walking.

I thought, "Oh God, I passed my street!"

I looked at my watch and it was almost ten o'clock. I thought, "Man am I in trouble! I know they know I'm gone by now."

I turned back around, still stoned. I started back toward home, and the next thing I knew I was back at her apartment.

I had missed my street again and walked all the way back to her house. By this time I was starting to come down. I don't know if the dope was laced, if it was exceptionally good dope or if it was the first time that I ever got high or what it was, but I was stoned. I thought, "This is it, buddy. I'll never touch any more of that stuff."

I finally got home and sneaked back in my bedroom. I didn't get caught.

Then the pressure was off so all the promises I made to God..., you know how that goes. The next day at school I was telling my friends, "Boy I smoked some bad dope last night!" — bragging, you know. I didn't tell them about the fears; how I'd missed my street two times and was late; how I'd got scared with this girl trying to get it on with me in the woods and everything. I didn't tell them any of that. Of course she told everybody. She blabbed how she wanted to get with me and how I was scared. She didn't tell them that I got paranoid because I was high. She said that I was scared to have sex. That caused a big scandal. I called her a liar and said, "Who wants to be with her!"

Her friends believed her and my friends believed me. It was really of no consequence. That was the first time I got high.

She was a year or two older than me, was probably used to getting high so she didn't understand why I wanted to get out of those woods so quickly.

I had some friends and I used to go to their house and smoke cigarettes. They were two or three years older than me.

We would hide in a ditch behind the house and get high. By the time I was in the eighth grade, these other guys were driving. They came down the street and they had a couple of six packs of beer yelling, "Come on Kelly, get in."

I had never drunk anything alcoholic, and one of the guys gave me two beers! He said, "Here, man, go ahead and drink these."

I slowly opened up a can and took a sip and said, "This doesn't taste bad."

So I swigged down those two beers. I got a buzz and thought, "Wow! Pretty good."

I was now on my way! I had smoked dope and learned that I could smoke it and enjoy it. I could drink beer and learned that I could enjoy it. So, I was really cool and accepted.

A rock concert was coming to town, and I was trying to make an impression and said, "Hey, guys, I'll bring some joints and treat us to a real high. What a blast it will be."

I had never been to a concert and there were some real

heavies coming. Mother's Finest and J. Guiles were going to be there. I had been telling all my friends, "Hey guys, no problem. I can get the dope."

Well, I had no idea where I could get any dope. So I tried to think of a thousand reasons why I couldn't go to the concert.

One of my older friends that gave us the beer came to me and said, "You know Nancy Carpen real well, don't ya, Kelly?"

"Sure," I answered. "Why do you want to know?"

Nancy was in my class at school and was exceptionally nice-looking, built, and overly mature for her age. "I want to meet her," he replied.

"Okay, let's make a deal. You get me some dope and I'll set you up with her," I said.

He got me a small bag of marijuana for $5.00 that would roll about ten joints. I strutted all the way to the concert.

In one moment, I built a reputation of being able to get dope. By the time I was fifteen, one year later, I was getting high every day of the week on Marijuana and getting drunk every night of the week on beer.

My friend John, whose father was a public official, and I stayed stoned. There was a guy up the street who was a lot older than us and always had good dope. I would do anything to get dope from him.

Dad had then been gone from home for years and lived in his trailer right outside town. One night he had a massive nosebleed and was rushed to the hospital. The doctor said if he had not had that hemorrhage, he would have had a severe stroke. They checked his heart and said he was on the verge of having a massive heart attack or a stroke any minute. They began to do extensive tests on him and found out that part of the reason for his high blood pressure was clogged arteries.

So he was having great, great difficulties. The doctor told him, "There is no way you can live by yourself; you'll die in your sleep."

Not knowing what else to do, he went back to live by himself. Several weeks later he had a heart attack, and they rushed him to the hospital. Afterward he needed help so he moved into our house, supposedly, temporarily. It was weird.

It was the first time my dad had ever lived at home on a consistent basis. He began to be the father and the head of the house. I didn't openly resent it, but I did resent it. By this time I was pretty wild and my mother was totally naive.

Because of her work schedule, she didn't know if I was coming or going. She had no idea I was getting high, getting drunk, and sneaking in and out. All at once I had a very strict dictator telling me what to do. I resented that since he had never been around. "What right," I thought, "did he have to come in and start telling me what to do?" As far as I was concerned, I was the man of the house. I didn't need him around. I never really talked back a lot to my mom and dad to their faces, but I did behind their backs.

Several months later he had major surgery on both legs for bypasses on major arteries in his legs. He was bedridden and I could see that it was going to be a permanent situation.

He'd never move out again. My poor, stupid, Christian mother (I thought) was just glad to have him back. One day she said to me, "Kelly, I know that your daddy never said it out of his mouth that he was sorry, but I could tell that he was trying to say it by all the things he has done for us. He built on to the house, he bought us a new car and all those types of things.''

I think she was right. I think he did want to say he was sorry, but for me, it was too late. It was just too late. I loved him and I didn't resent his being there, but I didn't want him telling me what to do or trying to be a part of my life. I would tolerate him but that was it. I guess your parents can hardly do anything to you to make you not love them at least in some form or fashion. If they could, I would not have loved my dad because he totally betrayed me in anybody's estimation, but I still loved him.

Ninth grade was my first full year in school that my dad was at home. He knew about my drinking and smoking but not about doing drugs. My tongue became a viper. I didn't cuss at my parents, but I cussed in front of them. With my dad every other word was filth and four letter words. That was his vocabulary and then it became mine.

God's name was constantly taken in vain. We didn't think anything of it. That was just part of our conversation. We would sit at the breakfast table, and I would talk about somebody and curse constantly. My folks didn't know what we were doing. They didn't know that I was staying stoned all the time. I had become dependent on drugs. Young people say, ''Well that's just what adults say.'' But I can tell you that I got high for three main reasons: It was the accepted thing to do and it made me popular and accepted in the circle of people I hung out with.

Secondly, I could get high and I could forget about everything until I had to come back home. I was not happy with my home situation even though I was part of a complete family. I was just not happy.

Finally, there was something missing in my life. I was

trying to fulfill some kind of desire by using drugs and alcohol and by sleeping with everyone I could.

The main reason why I ever started getting high was everybody else was doing it. Then I started to like getting high. I didn't start drinking beer because I liked the way it tasted. It was peer pressure. I wanted to be accepted, and it was the popular thing to do. Once I got into it, I started liking the buzz and the high, and that just compounded my problems. The national pastime of teenagers was and is partying. If you didn't party, there was nothing to do.

When I hit the tenth grade, my dad bought me a car. I really went wild. He bought me a 1970 GTO and it was sharp! I mean it was smooth and it was in perfect condition. A guy who owned an electronic shop had owned it. He was an older man, and he had taken perfect care of it so it was in mint condition. I would load the car up with dope and load the trunk up with beer. I was sixteen years old and living a "total party" lifestyle. We'd get drunk and stoned every night and pick up some girls and take them out parking.

There was a place called Sandy Creek outside town, a big concert ground where all the big bands would come. It was way outside the city limits so the police couldn't come there.

That was why it was so popular. ZZ Top came out there and did a big concert. Six of us went. It was my best friend's birthday, and his dad had just bought him a new Firebird. Our other friend was with us was too. We were like the three musketeers. We had our girl friends or whatever girls we were with. We decided to give John a bunch of Quaaludes as a birthday present. I gave him four and Jim gave him three.

John shouldn't have taken over two. He was drinking

and snorting a bunch of cocaine and no telling what else he was doing. After the concert he got in his Firebird, his girl friend with him, and peeled out of Sandy Creek. He was going back to Montgomery, which was straight down the highway. It was maybe fifteen miles out of town. He and his girl friend were alone in the car. There was a state trooper behind them.

The state trooper turned his radar on and clocked them going ninety-five miles an hour. John leaned over to kiss his girl friend, hit a bridge embankment, and flipped the car several times. The state trooper was right there and saw the whole thing. The car landed upside down about thirty feet down into a swamp of about a foot of water. John didn't get hurt and crawled out of the car. The girl's long hair was trapped under the car and she couldn't get out. The car was getting ready to burst into flames. The state trooper and John struggled frantically to get her out and managed to release her just moments before the car ignited.

After the accident report was written up, the trooper felt sorry for John because he had torn up his new car. He didn't even write him a ticket. John was drunk as a skunk. We picked him up after all the hullabaloo was over and went on partying. We were that stupid and that addicted to booze and dope. It was like nothing mattered; nothing else was important. It didn't matter that a new car was demolished. It didn't matter that two people almost lost their lives. It simply didn't matter. The only thing that mattered was staying high. John and his girl were upset for twenty or thirty minutes. We told them it was OK. The thing he was afraid of was telling his dad he tore up the car. It was not that they almost got killed or anything like that. We went back into town and scored some more dope.

I had a couple of pushers I got dope from. So it was easy.

We went back into town and finished the night up partying.

About four in the morning, I took everyone home and dropped into bed. That might have seemed a little bit unusual, but that was pretty much, the run-of-the-mill weekend — except for the totaled car.

Kelly age 6 at Lowneds Academy.
In a too big hand-me-down uniform.

5

ONE STEP DOWN

We would start about six o'clock and turn the music up in the car as loud as it would go. We'd start out with two or three six packs of beer, drink the beer till it was gone and then go get a couple of bottles of wine. We were all minors.

None of us were old enough to be buying booze, but there were places all over town where we could buy it. Sometimes we'd sit in front of a Jiffy Mart and see somebody twenty-one or twenty-two who looked pretty hip. We'd catch him and say, "Hey, man, get us some beer while you're in there."

They'd get us some beer and bring it out. There were places in town that didn't care to whom they sold the booze. They were closed down numerous times by the police for selling booze and liquor to minors. There was a town called Wall, Alabama, right out from town. We'd go up there every day. We could buy whiskey, wine, beer, or anything we wanted up there. It didn't matter if you were twelve, thirteen or fourteen years old. They didn't care. You could go in there with a big cooler and fill it up. Our average night was four or five of us guys getting together as friends, just guys — no girls. We'd get three or four six packs and we'd ride around.

We'd mostly ride up and down the Atlanta Highway, which was the cruising strip for Montgomery. We'd drink until we would get a pretty good buzz going. Then someone would say, "Anybody got any dope?"

"No. Let's go find some."

We'd ride around till we'd see somebody driving that we knew had dope. We'd pull them over and buy some dope, or go to a pusher's house and buy some. We would smoke a bunch of dope to get the night started real good.

We would drink up all the beer and smoke about a joint a piece after passing it all around. Then we were ready for sex." "Let's go find some girls!"

We didn't want to get the girls unless we had got some more dope. We'd have some pills, cocaine, more marijuana, and of course more beer. Then we would go to Crystals or just cruise.

Everybody had hot rods in those days. (Everybody is driving four cylinders these days, but back then everybody had hot rods). We would see some girls we knew or see some we didn't.

If they were by themselves, we'd pick them up. We'd all ride around and get high. The unspoken deal was: We ride you around and turn you on to our booze and dope and then we could have sex with you. I was sixteen years old, but some of the kids in the car were fourteen. The group of kids I hung around with didn't consider themselves bad. The girls were nice girls. We didn't consider them bad. We had sex with the girls but we didn't consider them sluts. They were just girls. We'd go park out in a field somewhere. I remember one night that John and I picked up two girls that we knew. It was freezing cold, man! It was in the dead of winter. After we snorted a bunch of coke, drank a bunch of beer and smoked some dope, John said, "There's nothing to do. What do you all want to do?"

"Well, let's go parking." one girl said.

John and I were so moral that we didn't want to make out in front of each other. That's how moral we were! So, it was like, who's going to get out? Both girls' names were Lisa.

We had to decide who was going to be with this Lisa and who was going to be with that Lisa? It didn't matter to us. Well, neither one of them wanted to choose and hurt our feelings.

So I said, "OK, let's flip a coin to see who gets who. That's the first step."

"Well, who's getting out? Let's flip a coin to see who gets out."

So one couple got the back seat of the car and the other couple was out on the cold ground in the middle of the winter; the girls were probably only fifteen!

It was a constant party. Then there were the weekend house parties. I can still see the names and the faces and even the furniture in those houses.

There would be hundreds of teenagers. There was a neighborhood called Arrowhood, which was one of the ritziest sections of town. By this time, I was selling dope. I would take a couple of grams of cocaine to a party on Friday night — which was everybody's payday — and cut it up into dimes or into $10.00 lines and sell it. I'd just line up a bunch of lines in the bathroom on a glass and put in on the back of the commode. I would cut up fifteen to twenty lines of cocaine, and they'd come in one at a time and give me their $10.00 and snort a line and go out. I'd take $50.00 worth of cocaine and make two or three hundred off of it. That's how I got started. "Man, it's so easy to make money like this," I thought.

One night I was at a party in Arrowhood. I was out there selling dope in the bathroom. A guy came to the party who was an acquaintance of mine. I knew him fairly well and owed him some money. We took a walk outside and I said, "I'm not giving you your money."

So we were standing face to face, getting ready to get in a fight. A guy was standing beside him who I didn't know.

Before I ever knew what was happening, this guy standing beside him cold-cocked me. I mean, he hit me like five times.

When I started to get up, he pulled this big hunting knife out of his boot and started to jump on me. I threw my feet up to stop him. Then a friend of mine standing there grabbed a big snow scoop out of the back of a pick up and WHAM, knocked this guy out. Someone took this guy to the hospital and he got over it. I had a big black eye and I was mad...but glad that I wasn't knifed. The guy I owed the money to was all apologetic and sorry that this guy had jumped on me. The money was forgotten about. That was like ten o'clock at night. We totally forgot about the fight. We went and drank a bunch more booze, did a bunch more drugs, and went to another party.

We were all at this other party in another neighborhood the same night. The guy who got hit with the shovel was released out of the E.R. He came over to this other party not knowing we were there. The party was going on in another big, rich neighborhood called Carrage Hills. All the people in that neighborhood went to Johnerson Davis High School, and all the people in my group went to Robert E. Lee High School. We were big rivals. We shouldn't have been over in that neighborhood anyway. We were over there because "We loved to party!" At those big parties, there would be a liquor table and a drug table. What you couldn't get free, you could always buy.

There was never a shortage. Montgomery was right above Mobile, which was a port city. Most of the drugs that go to Atlanta and Nashville come through Montgomery so drugs were always available.

The guy throwing the party was a big football star, and I weighed at least 135 pounds. He started mouthing off to me because I went to Robert E. Lee. I had on a big turquois ring that was about an inch-and-a-half around. I was about half drunk and he was drunk too so I said, "Look, man, I don't want any trouble from you."

What I really meant was, "I don't want to fight you because you're bigger than me."

If it had been the other way around, I'd have jumped on him quickly. I said again, "Look I don't want any trouble. I don't want to fight."

Just then this guy who had tried to stab me came walking up. He realized that he had jumped on me wrongly so he thought he owed me one. He said to the football player, "Why don't you leave Turner alone?"

The big guy said, "Who are you?"

He said, "It doesn't matter who I am. He's told you that he doesn't want to fight. Why don't you leave him alone?"

We were standing under the carport in the driveway at this big guy's house. This guy who just two hours ago had busted me in the eye was now standing there trying to stick up for me. So this big guy said, "Well why don't I just jump on you?"

He yelled, "You're not going to jump on me!" and

pulled his knife out again. This guy was knife-crazy. So he took a swing at this big 240-pound football player with his knife.

The football player took off running and screaming, "He tried to cut me; he tried to cut me."

He ran over to a pick up truck and got a tire tool and came running back. By this time Joe, the guy with the knife, was gone. I thought, "Man, what a night! Somebody is going to get killed before this night is over."

Most of these kids were in the upper-middle-class, living in $150,000 to $250,000 houses. God only knows where their parents were — maybe out partying themselves. These parties, man, happened every weekend. Two or three people had a party every weekend. "Where's the party this weekend?" was the big question. The party would be in somebody's house, and a hundred to two hundred teenagers would be there. Almost every weekend the police would come and raid a party. All the kids were high-schoolers, minors and too young to be drinking. There were thousands of dollars' worth of drugs at most parties every weekend. Nobody ever got taken to jail.

The police would come in and say, "You have to break this up. We've gotten a complaint. You're disturbing the peace."

Fifty or sixty cars would be parked on the curbs in a residential neighborhood, and the police did nothing about it.

Anyway, I'm thinking, "Man, somebody is going to get killed here tonight. These people are crazy."

Then it was twenty minutes later and we had totally forgotten about the tire iron. (When you're drunk and high, your attention span is short). We concentrated on what was happening right then. A group of us were standing out in the middle of the front yard. The guy called Joe who had the knife was standing there and we were all laughing, cutting up, and talking about how crazy the night had been. We were all stoned. Suddenly we hear an "Aaaagh!"

This football player came running out of the bushes as fast as he could, running full-speed all 240 pounds of him. And with a cracking sound, he whacked Joe right in the nose, busted his face open, and split his nose down the middle. Joe fell down on the ground, screaming, and kicking all around.

Somebody put him in a car and took him to the hospital for the second time that night. I told my friend, Brian, (the guy I was originally going to fight with) "I'll tell you what, it serves that Joe right. He tried to cut me earlier tonight and that's what he gets. I don't care if he was trying to take up for me, that's what he gets. He shouldn't have ever tried to cut me, he got it back."

Earlier that night I had seen Joe go upstairs with this Nick's girl friend. Nick was a big, macho Italian, and a friend of mine. Nick was out of town. I don't know what happened. I just saw them go in a bedroom together and the door was closed. The lights were out and they were up there for a while. The next day when I saw Nick, I said, "Nick, I'm not gonna add anything to this. All I'm going to say is that last night I saw Joe and Lila go upstairs together and lock the bedroom door. They were in there by themselves with the lights out. Now, Nick, don't tell Joe that I told you that."

Nick said, "OK, and you don't tell him I know."

Joe had been released from the hospital, and he was coming over to the apartment. When he walked in, we saw he had a plastic brace on his nose. It was all taped up and his eyes were black and blue. I mean his face was all messed up. He didn't know that Nick knew he had been with his girl friend the night before. He'd been hit with a shovel. He'd gotten his face all busted up by this 240-pound guy, and then Nick, this big Italian, was going to get him again, but Joe didn't know it.

We were in a second-story apartment. It belonged to some girl one of the guys was dating. We were all over there swimming and drinking beer. It was Sunday morning about eleven o'clock. I was sitting there punching John in the ribs saying, "Watch this. Nick is going to get him and he doesn't even know it."

Nick was acting cool like nothing had ever happened and like he didn't know anything. "Hey Joe!" Nick said, "You want to go with me to my grandmothers to do laundry?"

"Ya, I guess so; I don't have anything else to do," came the reply.

So Nick said, "OK, let me go get my laundry and I'll be right back."

He went toward the back of the house. Joe turned around and Nick ran up behind him and body tackled him running his face through a solid wooden door. Of course he just busted his face back open again, and Joe went over the top rail of the balcony. Nick let him go over. It was twelve feet down over that balcony! He landed hard. He was holding his face, which was all broken open again. The door was broken and the balcony rail was busted. It was a pretty wild weekend, but that was not totally unusual.

Another weekend, several of us were at another big party, and a bunch of guns started going off. Some dopers shot holes in all the ceilings and then ran outside chasing a guy and shot up his car. Then another guy unloaded a gun, seven bullets, in a house full of people.

Nobody got killed or hurt, but it was just miraculous that four or five didn't get killed.

That sounds like something out of a fiction story but it was not fiction. It was a frightening fact. It happens all the time in the average life of a regularly partying teenager into drinking beer, smoking dope, popping pills, snorting cocaine, and usually fighting or wrecking a car.

My dad bought me this GTO while I was totally into the partying scene. He was in the hospital because he had suffered several heart-attacks. I was a full-time student and I was not working. Most of the money I had, I had gotten from my parents or stolen from them. I could buy an ounce of good marijuana for $35.00 which would last me for a week if I smoked it on the average and didn't abuse it. Two bucks went for a six pack. So on forty or fifty bucks a week, I could stay high just doing mari juana, drinking, and taking a few pills. I also stole some vallium from my dad, a few at a time. When I would steal money, I would take it out of my mother's purse. My dad would give me ten bucks to get my big old German Shepherd dog a fifty-pound sack of dog food. I'd spend twenty minutes going up and down the grocery aisle so I could find a four-dollar bag of dog food. Then I would keep six bucks so I could buy beer with it. I had stolen money from my parents numerous times. I think they realized it one or two times, but I'd steal $5.00 or $10.00 at a time. They weren't looking for the thievery. By the time they had spent their money, they didn't know where it had all gone anyway.

Many times I'd tell them I'd lost a book at school and get them to give me more money. I couldn't think of all the things I have said to get money and to rip my parents off.

How I lied to them!

My drug habits were getting worse. I was starting to want to do speed and more cocaine, and I was smoking a lot more marijuana. I was wanting to be "Mr. Popularity" and throw big parties. I no longer was satisfied with six packs. I was buying kegs. Of course you don't buy a keg for $2.00 like you do a six pack. So I needed more money, and I started selling some drugs — just a little bit you know. I'd buy a quarter-pound of marijuana, cut it into four ounces, keep one, and sell the other three. I'd make enough profit to keep one.

Then I sold a couple of pounds. It got to where I bought enough speed (several hundred hits) at wholesale price and turned around and sold it to make money where I could stay high. One of my dealers told me, "Man, Kelly, snorting that cocaine is wasting it. You ought to start shooting that cocaine. Man, half of that stuff is getting stuck on the hair of your nose. You're not getting high enough for your money. You need to start shooting that stuff."

We were all starting to do a lot of chemicals. We were doing a lot of Crystal Meth — which was a granular type speed that you snort like cocaine. We were doing some Angel Dust, which is PCP. I didn't know the scientific name for it. (They used to use it for cattle tranquilizers but it's so potent that they don't use it on cows anymore. They use it on elephants. It comes in all different potencies, made in all different forms. They make it in the worst conditions imaginable). We got hooked on that PCP. We did that stuff for about a year, and I guess probably more people die from PCP than from acid.

(I don't know what the statistics are, but I know that it is dangerous because it is so unpredictable).

It was the summer after the tenth grade and my dad had lived at home for over a year. He had operations on both his legs. He was basically bedridden, but he was getting to where he could get around with a walker and a cane in the house. He was not working and was drawing 100% Social Security disability from the government.

My routine and schedule was pretty much settled, and I was used to my dad being there. I was not taking a lot of downers then, but I'd pretty much set the pattern for what was going to happen in the next two years in my life. It escalated and got worse.

John, Jim, and I decided to go to Florida. We always hung out together during late junior high and high school. We went to Fort Walton Beach to the Ramada Inn. It was a big, square luxury hotel with a courtyard in the middle. There was a big volcano-type thing with waterfalls which came off right in the middle of the pool. You could swim up under the waterfalls to a bar inside. Many of the Alabama high school and college kids went there on their senior trip or spring break. We were only eleventh graders, but we went down there to be part of the action!

We had an adjoining room with my pusher and three of his friends. He was always loaded with dope. He had a cap of a can of hair spray full of PCP. I mean that's enough dope to get a whole city high. It was the consistency of baking powder and light yellow. We decided we were going to shoot it, but we only had one dope needle.

In Okaloosa County, where we were, you couldn't get syringes o dope needles without a prescription. In Montgomery you could just walk in any drug store and grab a ten pack. We'd laugh and called it a family pack of syringes.

It was just like buying disposable razors. You bought a plastic bag full of them. In Okaloosa County, Florida, things were different. We tried everything to get more needles. We went to the pharmacy and the pharmacist said, "If you don't have a prescription for insulin or whatever, you can't get needles."

I said, "We don't have a prescription. My mother is at the hotel; we've got a poodle that is diabetic, and we have to have some syringes."

She smiled and said, "I'm sorry, sir, you've got to have a prescription."

We tried everything, and we couldn't get them. We did have one with us. I think it was a twenty-eight-and-a-half-gauge syringe and that was small. There were eight people there, so we decided we were going to shoot this PCP instead of snort it. (You can put it on your finger or put it in a drink or do anything, but we were going to shoot it and get the ultimate buzz). Seven of those guys used this needle. Now I mean this could have been hepatitis city, but luckily nobody caught anything, not even AIDS. It went around the circle. They were all shooting up. I was going to be last. By the time it got around to the fifth guy, the needle was getting so dull that when he forcedit into his skin you could hear it pop. When it got around to the seventh guy it broke off in his arm. Of course I couldn't use it. All seven of them OD'd on that stuff. I thought they would die. My best friend and my next-best friend were there. They all passed out. I thought they were dying. I didn't want the police to come in with all these guys dead and find me sitting there, so I ran. I left all of them. I left my friends for dead. I came back seven hours later to peek in and see if the police had been there or if they had died. They were starting to half-way come to.

Man, was I relieved. You would think we would have learned a lesson from that, but we didn't.

We were there for four weeks during the summer and

we did all of that PCP. We ran out of drugs. We ran out of money and we didn't even have gas money to get back home. We didn't have any food so two of these guys took a pistol and went down on the beach about five in the morning. They caught these people down there on the beach making out and robbed them. We stayed in Florida for several weeks by holding up people or stealing money from them. We'd get enough money to put gas in my car and then we'd drag race for money. We did anything for money. I mean **anything,** to get more dope.

Private school Kelly attended
through 3rd grade

Kelly age 15
His real hair

6

THE MURDER TRIAL

By the time I was seventeen, my life was tumbling like Texas sagebrush in a summer storm.

Thad lived on the same street as I did and we grew up together. He was kind of a strange and somewhat weird kid.

His parents were older, like my parents. Thad was a polite guy, but everybody thought of him as being rather unusual, even when he was a kid. Thad was nineteen so he was a couple of years older than me. When he turned eighteen, he had access to a trust fund, and he got his hands on a large sum of money. He started buying lots of drugs from me. By that time I had access to almost anything you could think of. I wasn't selling on a big scale, but a lot more than I ever had. I made enough money that I could stay high and still have money left over. I started selling him half-pounds and pounds of marijuana. That was a fairly large quantity for one person. He bought a lot of pills and he was taking quaaludes like candy. I mean Thad was eating pills, smoking dope, and snorting coke as quickly as I could get it. Anything that I could get, he would buy. He had all kinds of money to spend.

One Monday afternoon, on a real rainy March day, I was sitting in the driveway in my car and had the stereo turned up loud. It was raining so I knew nobody was going to come out of the house and since the windows were all fogged up, I lit up a joint in my car. Suddenly Thad knocked on the car window and I let him get in. There we were sitting in the driveway at my folks' house, and he said, "Kelly, Friday night I'm going to rob Skatehaven."

Skatehaven was a large skating rink not too far down the road from my parents' house. Thad had worked there and gotten fired. I said, "Look, man, don't tell me about it. I don't want to know about it. If the police come around here asking questions, I don't want to know anything. If you want to spend your money here, that's fine, but I don't want to hear about it."

He kept talking. I told him again I didn't want to hear it, but he went through all the details of how he was going to do it anyway. "I don't want to hear it!" That was my big line.

Finally he got out of the car and went home. Two days later, the weather was still rainy. I was sitting in the car again smoking a joint and getting high. Tap, tap on the window. There was Thad again and he got in the car with me.

He started telling me all over again, "I'm going down to Skatehaven Friday night, puncture the owner's tire and give him a flat. Then I will hide behind some bushes and when he bends down to change his tire, I'm going to knock him out and take the money bag."

I demanded, "Look, man, don't tell me anything about it!"

By then he had told me two times that he was definitely going to rob Skatehaven on Friday. On Friday evening about 6:30, I didn't have any gas in my car so I backed my car up to my sister's car and was going to siphon gas out of her car. While I was siphoning gas, Thad walked up and asked, "Hey, Kelly, will you drop me off at Skatehaven?" as he pulled his shirt up showing his gun stuck in his pants.

I said, "Man, I'm not going to drop you off anywhere. I know you're going to rob that place. No way am I gonna give you a ride down there."

Just about that time my dad came out, caught me siphoning gas out of the car, and demanded, "What are you doing?"

He got real mad and put me on restriction and sent me into the house. I couldn't go anywhere that night. If Dad hadn't been living at home, I probably would have ended up taking Thad down there, dropping him off and being an accomplice.

Saturday morning my father and I went down to Benton to check on the little house we owned where I grew up. We were renting it out. On the way I was listening to the radio when suddenly I heard, "We interrupt this program with a news bulletin. Last night Skatehaven Roller Rink was robbed and two employees were killed. It appears they were shot for no reason, in cold blood. No names are being released until the next of kin are notified."

I immediately thought I would pass out. It was the weirdest feeling I've ever felt. I was traumatized and I immediately got nauseated, I mean, instantly. I knew that Thad had murdered those two boys in cold blood. I knew it. I didn't say anything to Dad. My dad didn't really hear it. He thought the skating rink simply got robbed. Twenty minutes later when I finally could talk, I said, "Look, Dad, you're not going to believe what I'm fixing to tell you, but I swear it's the truth. I know what I'm talking about. I know who killed those boys."

"Who killed what boys?" he calmly asked.

"Skatehaven was robbed last night and two boys were killed and I know who did it."

"You're crazy." he replied.

"No, I'm not, Dad. Thad killed those boys. He told me two times this week that he was going down there last night to rob it," I shouted.

So my dad was real quiet and finally he said, "OK, OK."

When we got to Benton, we had to work on the water pump. I couldn't concentrate on anything. I was sick. I didn't know what to do. I'd never been in a situation like that. I was shaking like a leaf in a summer storm. Finally, we got the pump fixed and headed home All the way back to Montgomery, not one word was spoken between my father and me. My father was out of bed then and walking with a cane, but the only kind of relationship we had was a work relationship. Our relationship was getting a little better. Some of the resentment was leaving me, but my drug habit was getting worse. When we got home, I was thinking, "Dad doesn't believe what I just told him."

As soon as we stepped in the den, he said, "Kelly, are you sure that you know that Thad robbed Skatehaven and murdered those boys?"

I said, "Yes, he did Dad. I know he did it."

"What do you want to do, Kelly?" he asked.

I said, "I want to call the police."

"Well, I don't want to get involved, so I'll call Secret Witness."

We called Secret Witness and, of course, the lines were jammed. Secret Witness was a police number you could call if you didn't want to identify yourself to give an anonymous tip. I was scared out of my wits. "Dad, nobody else knows this. He will kill me too."

Thad rode a motorcycle and I saw him come in and go out of his drive. We tried to get Secret Witness again. Still the line was busy. My heart was pounding so hard I thought it would break my chest. I could hardly breathe. "Dad, I'm loading the shotgun, and I'm sticking it under the sofa in the living room. If that boy comes across the street, I'm shooting him because he's crazy," I whispered.

Finally we got through to Secret Witness, and Dad said, "Thad Kelso who lives at 1715 Dogwood Drive killed the two boys at Skatehaven Skating Rink last night."

As fast as he could, he hung up the telephone. After awhile, we saw the police detectives pull up. The detectives went to his house and knocked on the door. He was not there then. He was at his girl friend's house. They simply said to his mother, "We're here for Thad."

"For what?" she asked.

"To question him about the Skatehaven murders," they told her.

She called his girl friend's house and informed Thad, "Two detectives were here to talk to you."

Of course she didn't suspect him of doing it. He used to work there and she thought they wanted to question him about something else. The police were not very smart, as they tipped him off they were looking for him. Thad came home and the police came back later and picked him up. They took him downtown, questioned him for two hours, and then let him go.

He came back home. Thad was a crazy who had killed two kids the night before and he knew I turned him in. When his mother called over to his girl friend's house, Thad said to his girl friend then, "Oh my God! Kelly turned me in."

Of course I didn't know he had been released until later.

He came home and spent the night. From eleven o'clock that night until six o'clock the next morning he was free. At six o'clock the next morning, the police were at his house to pick him up. They charged him with a double murder. I didn't know why they had even let him out, but it sure was stupid. I didn't know at the time that he was out. He could have done anything during that time. Had I known he had been out, I would have been crazy with fear. We thought that once he had been arrested, that was it.

I don't know how they knew I had called, but somehow they apparently found out. The police came to my house on Sunday morning and asked, "Are you Kelly Turner?"

I said, "Yes, I am." (Of course I was still a minor.)

They asked, "Did you or your father call the police station last night about Thad Kelso?"

"Yes, we did."

"Could you come with us down to Skatehaven to look around?"

I looked at my dad, and Dad said, "Well, I guess you can. What does he have to do?"

They said, "We just want him to walk around with us, look around and see if he recognizes anything and answer some questions. Maybe he can give us some leads. We'll have him back in an hour."

"Well," my dad said, "I guess that will be all right.

Do you want me to go with you, Kelly?'' Dad asked.

I said, "No, it sounds simple enough; I'll go by myself."

I got in the detective's car. They took me up to the Atlanta Highway. They should have taken a right to go to Skatehaven, but they took a left and went toward downtown.

They took me downtown and had me down there for three hours of interrogation. They thought I was a party to the robbery and murders. I smoked like a fiend and they wouldn't even give me any cigarettes. They treated me like they just knew I had something to do with it. I finally cussed them out, calling them every name in the book and told them what they could do with their police station. "Lock me up; I'm not talking to you so and so's anymore. I felt like I was helping you and now you are doing me like this. I want to call my father. I want to call a lawyer. I'm not talking to you anymore."

They said, "You're not calling anybody."

Eventually, after they didn't bring me back home, my father tried to find out what happened. I had been to the police station plenty of times before. I had been arrested for public drunkenness and possession. One time I had a cigar box full of speed in tablet form. I was at this place called Cut Street where a lot of young people used to meet and cruise. I was riding with another guy and the police came and surrounded us. I was a minor. So all they could get me for was possession with intent to sell, but they couldn't do anything about it.

I'd been arrested for fighting a couple of times. It had been little small things. I'd just been picked up and let out in two or three hours. This time was different. This was serious. They had a totally different tone of voice. These weren't the second-year flunky detectives. There were several of them surrounding me. They were shooting questions at me from every side. Before I could finish one, they'd hit me with another.

Then my dad came in and said, "This boy is a minor, and he's not answering any more questions."

They had hit me with a barrage of questions for two or three hours. They treated me like a criminal. They had gotten me out of bed and taken me downtown. They wouldn't give me any cigarettes or anything to eat or drink. But when my dad protested that I was a minor, they finally let me go.

My mother was somewhat in the dark about everything I had been involved in. My father tried to protect her when I had been picked up for drunkenness, etc.

My mother never did totally catch on. She thought that I had eye problems because my eyes were always red. She never knew it was because I was stoned or drunk. She didn't know while Thad was locked up in the county jail, I received a call from a girl one night giving me a death warning.

We went through the preliminary hearings and I had testified against Thad in court. He had been there with his mom and dad. The parents of the murdered boys were there as well. It was a full-fledged trial and Thad still went back to the county jail.

There was a guy in there with him. I think his name was Joe Sina. Everybody on the street knew him as Barfly. They also knew he was crazy and carried a gun. He wasn't only mean, he was a lunatic. As a matter of fact, he is in the insane asylum today.

This death-warning call came about three or four months after they had arrested Thad. The girl was hysterical. I hadn't seen Lori in a long time, but I sure remembered her.

She had been a good friend. When Joe Sina got out of jail, he came over to her house because he knew her older brother. He was in the next room telling Lori's brother about this guy named Kelly Turner who narced on Thad and got him put in prison. He informed her brother that Turner was going to get wasted. Joe continued, "Thad told me that he drives a yellow GTO, rides down the Atlanta Highway to school, and lives on Dogwood Drive. He is 5 ft. 8 in. and has black hair."

Thad had told him everything about me. He had told him the directions I drove, what my car looked like, where I lived, who my parents were, everything. Lori overheard it through the door and called me. "Kelly, tomorrow he's going to be waiting for you on the Atlanta Highway. He has a gun and he's going to kill you. He's going to shoot you when you drive by. I heard him tell my brother this," she cried.

I decided to skip school after the call. I found out Joe Sina had a pistol and ran through the halls of Lee High School screaming, "Where's Kelly Turner, where's Kelly Turner?" The police aid of our school of 4,000 students had chased him. He had had a gun and ran out of the end of the building and got away.

The next day I went the back way to school, and I came up behind Joe and saw him standing in the median of the Atlanta Highway. It was raining and cold. He had no shirt on. One of his pant's legs was torn off above his knees, and he had a bandana wrapped around his forehead. Joe looked like a maniac. He had to be stoned. He was out there karate-kicking at cars. He didn't see me because I bypassed him and kept going. I took my sister and friends on to school. We all got out and went in the school just like any other day. Of course we were high. I didn't tell them about Joe because I didn't want them to

even know about it. As soon as the bell rang I left
school, got in my car and went home. "Dad," I said,
"There's a crazy man up on the Atlanta Highway trying
to kill me. Somebody called me and tipped me off. It's
not a joke! I sneaked up behind him on the way to
school and I saw him. He's up there on the highway."

Dad picked up the phone and called the police. When
the police picked Joe up, they already had a report on
him. To compound all this, like this wasn't wild enough,
I started getting strange phone calls. I would answer the
phone and all I would hear was somebody breathing
hard.

I would say, "Hello, hello," and they wouldn't say
anything. So I would hang up. This happened at ten
o'clock in the morning, six o'clock in the morning, three
o'clock in the morning, two o'clock in the afternoon,
five o'clock in the evening. The phone rang every time of
the day or night. This went on for three or four months.
If I picked up the telephone, they would hang on the
line. If my mother or father picked it up, they would
hang up. I knew the calls were for me. Finally we had the
phone tapped. We knew it was related to Thad's case.

My parents' lives would have been a lot more serene
without me. I had been in and out of court testifying at
least ten times. The entire time I was still doing drugs
and getting worse. My father's health was getting worse
and worse. He had a couple of heart attacks during the
trials. The phone calls were driving us crazy. We all
thought I was going to be murdered. At long last, they
traced the phone calls. It was a girl that I had stood up
on a date and she was bonkers. The entire family was
panicked because we thought it was some nut related to
my turning Thad in for murder. Every time a phone call
came, our whole family would jump. The girl just

wanted to hear my voice. I didn't know what her deal was. It was weird, but quite a relief. We all sat back and had a good laugh even though it "hacked us off." The calls had put us through such great stress, it was a great relief to laugh.

Being the key witness against Thad, I received a very large reward from the state for turning him in. Governor George Wallace posted a separate reward for each one of the boys. I had turned him in and testified against him. He was sentenced to death by electrocution. We got 75% of the reward. 25% went to the attorney for getting it.

My dad put a percentage of it in the bank and the rest in a trust fund for me. When I turned eighteen, I blew every nickel of it on drugs, parties, and booze. I didn't have guilt about Thad's sentence. I had wished they would have electrocuted him on the spot. I would have felt a lot safer.

My life continued its spiral downward.

Kelly and Kim's 16th birthday
Their father L. M. Turner

7

CODE OF ETHICS

John, Jim, Brian, and I all turned seventeen years old. We had all gotten fake ID's and were hitting certain bars that would let us in. We were drinking pretty regularly at the bars.

One particular occasion, we decided to go to a place called Cowboys. It was a lounge on top of the Holiday Inn. We had just left another bar called the Speakeasy which was a disco-dance-type place. They sold canned beer at the Speakeasy so we took several beers and were drinking on the way to Cowboys. To reach Cowboys you had to go up an elevator to the Penthouse. The other guys went up on the first load, and I stayed in the lobby talking to friends. The elevator came back down and I went up with the second load. When I got to the Penthouse, the doors opened, and four guys came shoving Brian back into the elevator. They were beating him and hitting on him, trying to stuff him back in the elevator.

They didn't have on name tags or uniforms so I didn't know they were employed by Holiday Inn.

They were a couple of bouncers: a bar tender and the manager. Brian had walked into the lounge with his can of beer, and the manager had walked over and said, "Son, you can't have that can of beer in here; you're going to have to throw it away." (They only sold bottled beer at Cowboy's.)

Brian said, "I'll drink it real quick."

He said, "No sir, you're going to throw it away."

Brian then took the beer and poured it all over the manager. Brian, of course, was drunk. As soon as he did that, the bartender jumped out from behind the bar, and two big old mashers and the assistant manager grabbed Brian.

Then there they were stuffing him back into the elevator! They were taking him downstairs to throw him out. I thought they were just a bunch of guys ganging up on my friend so I picked the littlest one (which happened to be the bartender) and hit him a couple of times and knocked him down. There was a handrail around the inside of the elevator, and I had a hold of his hair beating his head on that metal rail. The bouncers finally pulled me off the bartender. The police were called and we were all arrested and taken to jail. I told them, "I thought it was six guys jumping on my friend. I didn't know they worked here."

I was booked on assault with intent to do bodily harm. Then they reduced it to criminal trespassing. I told the judge, "Your Honor, to be criminally trespassing we would have had to have been there before and they would have had to tell us not to come back. We have never been there before."

So we got off with a slap on the hand. We got in one fight after another. I got put in jail for driving while intoxicated two or three times. (The penalties were not as stiff back then as they are now.)

At seventeen, an average day in my life consisted of waking up and getting out of bed by seven o'clock, getting ready for school, leaving for school at 7:30, and smoking a joint on the way. I would pick up John and my girl friend. We would ride around, drink a couple of six packs, and go to school.

After first period class was over, I'd go to the bathroom and smoke a joint before second period and third period. During lunch we'd skip eating and ride around getting high. We would come back to school and get high again in the bathroom. After school, I'd get with a bunch of guys and ride around town all afternoon, snort some coke, do pills, drink beer, smoke dope, and then find the girls.

The dope gave me all kinds of different feelings. I was doing uppers, downers, drinking, smoking dope, and shooting up for whatever feeling I wanted. If I took too many downers and was too tired to party, I'd do some speed. If I got too wired, I'd take some downers. If I drank and started to get too drunk to walk, I'd take some more speed. It was just a twenty-four hour cycle. If it hadn't have been for sleep, my body would never have gotten a rest from the drugs.

We saturated our bodies with drugs. Every teenager I knew in the culture and society I hung around with was a party animal. Everybody did it. I might have done it in excess, but as far as I knew, everybody did it — the girls and the guys. So we were just average young people. The guys who ended up being doctors, lawyers, attorneys, and cops did it too.

There were some kids who didn't. A boy named Lowell Mimms was "Mr. Straight." He had a plastic hairdo with never a hair out of place. I hated his type.

When he saw me coming down the hall, he moved to the other side. His kind were few-and-far-between, and I thought they were weirdos. I thought they were stupid. I was cool and knew what was happening. I was the one who had it all together.

In twelfth grade, my dad had some more operations. After another heart attack, his health began to really fail. My grandmother died in 1969 when I was very young. I was fairly close to her. She died the day the astronauts landed on the moon. My granddad didn't die until years later, when he was 96. I was just semi-close to him. My dad's health was very grave, but I didn't think he was going to die because I couldn't really relate to dying. I had not had anybody really that close to me die. Halfway through the twelfth grade, my dad had another heart attack and was in the hospital.

During that time I was called into the school office one day. I was told I had been expelled because I had skipped twenty-one days in a row. I had to go to the hospital and tell my dad and mom that I was expelled from school and wasn't going to graduate. (They were fools to do everything for me that they did. I would have washed my hands of me long ago. Man, it was some kind of trouble day in and day out, day in and day out.)

The next day I drove home at five o'clock in the morning from a poker game, drunk on Miller Ponies. It was storming and pouring down rain. I couldn't see ten feet in front of me and ran my car into a bridge embankment at seventy miles an hour. I totalled it and walked away without a scratch. I hitched a ride home with a policeman. He simply took me home and dropped me off. (I was always pulling stunts like that.) I put my parents through hell my teenage years. They knew that I smoked dope and later they knew I took pills. Dad had noticed that I had stolen some of his vallium. They also discovered that I had stolen money from them. Dad had several bank bags full of silver dollars and fifty-cent pieces. I had been stealing them three or four at a time over a period of years. One day he noticed they were all gone. He accused me, and of course I denied it — which was senseless. I was out of school, so they put me into Williams Preparatory School, which was a private school. It seemed to be where everybody else who had been kicked out of school attended. When I got there, I heard some kids hanging out of windows yelling, "Hey, there's Turner, there's Turner!"

My father turned to my mother and said, "Oh no, here we go again."

He immediately realized that I was going out of the frying pan and into the fire. They didn't know what to do. My dad was sixty-four, and my mom was in her late fifties. They just didn't know how to handle or cope with the kind of problem child I had become. They didn't relate to it. They were helpless and totally at the mercy of God to deal with the problem. They tried to talk to me. My father even resorted to sitting down with me and asking, "Kelly, what is the problem?"

I responded, "Don't hassle me! There is no problem. I can handle it myself."

My mother tried to love the problem out of me and would say, "Kelly, we love you. Can't you see that you are destroying your life? Don't you see that you are destroying your family? Don't you see that we've invested thousands of dollars to get you out of jail, thousands of dollars in your education? You have torn up two cars. Kelly, we love you, but there has got to be an end to this. There's got to be an answer. Honey, what is the solution? Don't you want to help yourself?"

I understood to a degree, but it seemed I was helpless to help myself. I wanted out but didn't think there really was an out. I couldn't see an alternative lifestyle. I continued to say my prayers every night. Oh yea, I had always said my prayers...always. I knew I was in adverse circumstances, but I didn't know I was enslaved and imprisoned by them.

I soon realized I could make some real money selling stolen guns. Another guy had stolen them, and I bought them from him at a wholesale price and resold them. There were people who came to my house at three or four o'clock in the morning to buy guns. They would get in a fight, get mad, need a gun, and come to my house. I didn't care who got shot or who got killed as long as I got my money for the guns. The only gun I knew for a fact caused somebody to get killed was one I sold to a sixteen-year-old. He in turn sold it to a fifteen-year-old. The kid who bought it walked out of his bedroom into the den and said to his sister and boy friend, "Look, I got a new gun."

He took a bullet, put it in the chamber, closed it, spun the chamber, and said, "Russian Roulette!"

With a loud boom, the first shot blew his brains out and killed him. My only remorse, my only concern, was not that this boy was dead or that his sister saw him get killed. I didn't want the gun traced back to me. I told the kid who I had originally sold it to, "If the police ask you anything about the gun, and you tell them anything about me, I'll kill you or have you killed."

It didn't really bother me. My conscience was calloused and I had become a hardened person. I was concerned only about Kelly Turner making money, doing my own thing, and enjoying life regardless of who it hurt.

Sexual immorality didn't bother me as something

wrong. The stealing and doing drugs were illegal, but they didn't make me feel like a bad person. I was still Kelly the good boy from a lower-middle-class family with a good Christian mother who was pretty much respected in my neighborhood. I did some work at construction. I got involved in helping build a Wendy's restaurant. The superintendent and foreman on the job bought dope from me. I hung around with them after work and went to their apartments. They took me into their confidence and told me about an embezzlement scandal going on. They were taking half the crew and remodeling houses and paying them out of the B and S Food accounts. Part of the crew was working on Wendy's while part of the crew worked on remodeling jobs being paid by Wendy's. Soon they were caught and busted. But it was those guys who taught me I could sell drugs to adults — not only just to teenagers. The older people had money and could buy high-quality drugs — in quantities. There was an attorney who saw me working out at the national guard base. He was building a store and approached me about helping him after school and on weekends.

I went to work for him. One day he broke the ice and asked me, "Kelly, do you get high?"

I said, "Yea, I get high."

"Can you get us some dope?" he asked.

I said, "Sure, what do you want?"

He said, "Take off an hour and get me some smoke."

So I got him some dope and we smoked it and got high. He introduced me to several other prominent people in town. I found out this whole circle of people were bisexual. They were very upper class people who had a lot of money. They did a lot of drugs and threw big parties and I sold the drugs to them.

My poor parents! How they put up with the endless antics of this idiot kid of theirs! They even took me to an analyst.

They asked, "What's wrong with him? Is he crazy? Is he stupid? Does he have a below-normal IQ? What's his problem?"

The analyst retorted, "No, he's got an average IQ. He's not crazy and he's not hyper-active. He's not below average. I can't tell you anything. Apparently he just doesn't want to do right."

I was never afraid anyone would blackmail me because of the code of ethics. In the drug sub-culture, no one turned you in. The same was true even with the adults. If I sold them drugs and they walked out and got busted, they wouldn't tell where they had gotten them. Even among the "goof balls" who were involved in it held to a certain unspoken code of ethics. You understood a set of principles and rules that you went by if you wanted to live. Somebody would kill you for narcing on them.

I knew I was a black sheep, and I knew I was putting my parents through a lot. I really didn't understand their concern. The only thing I was concerned about when I was kicked out of school was the "butt chewing" that I was going to get. All I wanted to know was how long I'd be grounded. It was that flippant. I guess I was kind of a con man too. Even when the discipline wasn't my biggest concern, I would act like it was to my parents. I didn't want to say, "I'm sorry that I'm putting you through all this."

My honest-to-God feeling when I got expelled from school was total failure. It was another blow to my parents and still another time that I proved I could be a disappointment to them. I had a very poor self-image.

But man, when I had that money for turning Thad in and had the drugs and two kegs of beer in the trunk of my car, I wasn't a failure! I had friends around me! I was "Mr. Popularity" when I had all the drugs. When I sold them, I had people coming to me and I was important. There were lots of reasons why I did the things that I did. There were insecurities, the need to be accepted, the desire to be somebody, not to be a failure but be important, to be needed, to be wanted, to be respected and looked up to. That was a very, very important part of it.

Parents need to instill in their kids who they are. If they always tell them they are stupid, or they can't make it, then the kids feel "What's the use?" I felt I could never please my dad. My dad was a negative person. He wasn't a mean person but my insecurities and need to be accepted came from the lack of acceptance from my dad. That was a hundred per cent of it.

When I was having sex, I didn't feel I was getting love. I felt I was staying up to par with a lot of the other guys who were getting a lot of sex. It was like another notch in the gun. "Well I had sex with so and so and you haven't yet," or "I've had sex with just as many as you have."

I stayed up to par with the rest of the guys. That was number one. Secondly, I just liked the sex. Thirdly, it was the feeling of dominance that kept me going...I tricked you so I'm smarter than you. That was a big part of feeling like I had conquered. There was definitely no love involved. I had been after this and I had outwitted them.

We were persistent. The guys would do things two or three times until the girls quit saying, "Don't do that."

Then a hand would go on their back end and there was a little bit of resistance, but guys just chipped away at them.

Finally, when a guy got a girl in bed, he'd think, "You're so dumb. You should have seen this coming two weeks ago when I started out flattering you."

The harder they were to get in the bed, the bigger the conquest was and the bigger the thrill. There was never the sense that this girl loved me or this girl cared about me because I didn't care. I just liked the sex and I liked being able to say that I had sex with this person. I even liked it if I had to lie and say, "Well she wasn't that good," because then I was the judge.

8

TWO DEATHS

I was dealing a lot of drugs. I was selling drugs to the thirteen, fourteen, and fifteen-year-olds. I didn't make a lot of money, but enough to do all the drugs I wanted to and maybe clear a hundred or so a week. That was a lot of bucks for a seventeen-year old. Some weeks I would lose money and go into the hole because I'd get with a bunch of friends and turn them all on to the drugs. I met Rene during a time like that.

Rene's parents had owned a Cadillac Continental dealership.

Her father had died of a heart attack in his forties and was very wealthy. Her mother liquidated all the assets and moved to Montgomery. This girl was ugly. When I say this girl was ugly, I mean this girl was ugly. She looked like a boy. She had no shape and had a big, funny-looking nose. To top it off, she didn't know how to fix her hair. She did, however, have a lot of money. I could tell that by the clothes she wore and the car she drove. Immediately, I found that she got high. I made sure she knew I had a lot of drugs.

We started going out; not as a date, but just driving around. I'd sell her drugs and she'd turn me on to it. I'd sell her a hundred dollars' worth of coke. I'd do fifty of it and she'd do fifty of it. That went on for a month.

One day, about three o'clock, we left school together in her car. We left my car parked at the dead-end by the school parking lot. We rode around and came back at seven o'clock that night. The police were sitting there and blocked us off.

A detective got out and came up to the car. It was storming and raining "cats and dogs." There was lightning and thunder — the whole works. He said, "Look, Turner, we don't even want to get out and search you and the car. We've busted you before. We've got you this time and we'll catch you again. Just give us what you have and we'll let you go."

I said, "All right" and gave him an ounce of dope and five quaaludes.

He said, "Tell your girl friend to do the same thing."

I said, "Rene, this detective says if you give him what you've got, he'll let you go."

She said, "Ok" and gave him a small film container that had six quaaludes.

He then said, "All right, you can now let me check your purse real quick."

Of course when he checked her purse, he found seventy-five.

I had sold her eighty quaaludes that day. They took her in and let me go. She told them that she had gotten the quaaludes from me (which she had). They made a deal that they would let her go if she would set me up. She didn't come back to school for about two weeks. When she did come back, she told this big story of how much trouble she had gotten in.

She explained her probation. She still had to go to court and didn't know what was going to happen. I steered clear of her and forgot her.

I laughed about it and said, "She's stupid; she got busted and I didn't. She got busted because she was greedy and tried to hold out on the cops. If she had given them all the ludes, they would have let both of us go."

I was over half-way through the last semester of my twelfth grade. We had already ordered caps and gowns and our class rings when I was called out of class to come to the phone.

The voice on the other end was quick and to the point: "Kelly, this is Dr. Smith. You need to come to the hospital at Maxwell right away."

I asked, "What is it?"

He said, "It's your dad."

"Is he all right? What's happening?" I questioned.

He said, "You need to come out here as fast as you can."

I believed it was pretty bad. I jumped in the car and went to Max Air Force Base Hospital. I had known that dad was going to the hospital for a check up. So I was surprised to get a phone call.

When I arrived, Mom said, "Kelly, your dad has had a massive heart attack. He left the hospital and was driving home when this attack hit. They had just told him everything was all right. I have called Kim."

"Mom," I asked. "Is dad going to die?"

"As he was having his attack," she continued, "an off-duty state trooper saw him swerving all over the interstate.

He saw your dad's car pull off on the side of the interstate and saw your dad fall over. The trooper pulled in behind him and said that your dad could barely talk by that time. He got the words out, 'Take me back to Maxwell Hospital.' The trooper got him back here and they have put an external pacemaker on him.''

My twin sister was already in college, and my next oldest sister had already graduated from college. Here I was the only boy in the family, and my dad wasn't going to see me graduate. I was on a guilt trip but didn't even understand it was a guilt trip. If I had been bad up to that time, I went to hell after that. I literally, totally went to the dogs. I didn't talk to anybody. I was a person with very little emotion. My brother-in-law and I had walked up to the canteen of the hospital. When we came back, my other brother-in-law had just come through the doors and said, "Kelly, Im sorry. Your dad is gone."

I knew what he had said, but I didn't cry. I didn't do anything. I turned around and walked off. I loved my dad in my own way. My only thoughts were, "I've let him down."

I felt that my dad had died of a broken heart because of the chain of events that had happened over the last few years. I believed my father had given up the will to live.

Dad was dead, I thought, because he had seen no hope in me.

I should have been in the penitentiary. I should have been killed, as much crazy stuff as I had done. I called Kim and she was still at school. I wanted to be by myself so I said, "I'm going down to Troy to pick up Kim."

I went down to Troy, which was fifty miles south of Montgomery, and drove up in front of her dorm. She came out and got in the car. I didn't say, "Hi, how are you?" Nothing! We drove an hour back to Montgomery. Never was a word spoken between us. We got to the house and I went to my bedroom. I didn't communicate with my mother. I didn't communicate with my sisters or my family or my relatives or anybody over the next few days. I wasn't belligerent about it. I simply didn't enter into any conversation. I didn't want to help pick out the casket or anything. I wanted to stay by myself. I didn't cry with my mother or say I was sorry. I was afraid of my emotion.

I stayed pretty much to myself. I didn't know what happened to my sisters. I was unaware of what they were doing or how they were reacting. The only request that I made was that they put the flag on the casket and and that I could have it.

I didn't want to go to the funeral parlor. I told my mother, "I'm not going down there to view the body."

Dad never needed anyone. I didn't want to face it. I didn't want to see my dad dead. I didn't want to see my dad helpless in a casket. There was a big 6 ft. 4 in. black guy named Jessie Powell who had worked for my dad for years and was a part-time preacher. He came to me and said, "Come on with me, Kelly. We'll go down there together."

So I went with him to the funeral home and viewed the body.

That kind of broke my fear, and I was able to deal with the fact that I had to go to the funeral. I was of no comfort to my mother or my sisters. I was very quiet and stuck a little closer to home than I usually did. I had been an alley cat at night. I prowled quite a bit when the sun went down, being gone till one or two o'clock. I didn't go to school for a week and totally cut myself off from the kids at school. They sent flowers and some would call but I wouldn't talk to them.

The only time I spent with my mother was at the

funeral when I walked in with my arm around her and sat beside her. The funeral was at the funeral home, not at a church. I kept my arm around her and remember pulling her up closer to me just when they brought in the casket. That was my moment of truth.

I hugged her a little bit after the funeral. I hadn't been scared to hug her, but I wasn't a huggy, touchy type person.

That was the only consolation I had for anybody — a little embrace for my mother.

I had cousins up from Florida. One of the guys was a teenager about my age. My friends, John and Jim, were also there. When we got home from the funeral, the first thing we did was go in my bedroom, pull out the coke tray, and snort up about two or three grams of coke. Then we went out and rode around and smoked dope. We didn't talk about the funeral or about my dad's death. It was just like nothing had happened. I ignored it.

I went back to school a few days later. I didn't want those people to pat me on the back or tell me, "I'm sorry."

I just wanted to act like nothing had happened. That was the way I was acting. That was the way it happened to a degree. I guess they sensed that I didn't want to talk about it. I just didn't want them to bring it up. I wanted to act like it had never happened. I just wanted to go on with my life. I wanted to be fun-loving, party animal Kelly. I guess I thought to admit I had sorrow, remorse, or a broken heart would have made me less than a man. I was always cool. I was always there. I always had the drugs. I never thought about anybody. I wanted to maintain that non emotional macho image.

That was pretty much how I wanted it to stay and it

pretty much did. Nobody after the first day said anything to me about my dad, and I never said anything to them. I just kind of forgot all about it. I just let it go. It was no big deal.

There was a lot of guilt and a lot of pressure and all kinds of crazy emotions that happened to me from the time my dad died to the time I graduated. I just went down, down, down. I started getting stoned twice as much and started staying out later at night doing worse things. I totaled three cars in the next six months before I graduated. I would leave home and stay gone for two or three days.

My mother helped me buy a new car. It wasn't brand new but it was new to me. It was a '78 Mustang. I got a new stereo to put in it and everything. My mother and I came home from a trip to North Carolina to visit my Uncle. I went over to my friend Brian's house and put in the stereo. Several guys I ran around with were there. Somebody said, "Let's all go to Florida."

That was on a Sunday afternoon. We split and went to Florida. We didn't say anything to anybody. We were all still in high school, but it was during spring break so we didn't have to go to school the next day. We planned to go down there and party that afternoon and come back that night. The closest beach was only about three or four hours from Montgomery. Somehow we got involved in a big party down there and didn't get back until seven o'clock the next morning. My mother had lost it. She called the police because she didn't know where I was. I left Sunday afternoon to put a stereo in my car and didn't come home. My car was gone and I was gone.

All my friends were gone. So where were we? The police were out looking for us.

This had happened numerous times. I would go to the

store and wouldn't come home. The next day, I'd show up at mid-morning drunk or stoned while the police had been out looking for me all night. Mom would be thinking I had been in a wreck or had gotten my throat cut or gotten killed in a dope deal.

I was supposed to be at work at eight o'clock that morning.

I came staggering in at seven o'clock, drunk, and high after partying all night in Florida. My mother made me go to to work. I was a part-time truck driver, delivering furniture. I was in no condition to work, but I went to work thinking I could work a half a day and then manage to slip into the back of the truck and go to sleep. I managed.

I was like that the next couple of months. I finally graduated. I had one summer off and then I started going to John Patterson Technical College where I took up welding. The guys I was in school with were mostly drunks and partiers that wanted to get high or stoned. It was better for me because a lot of them were veterans who were going back to school on their G.I. bill. Some of those guys had been to "Nam". They knew how to do the big drugs like acid and heroin. They didn't have to go home to Mom and Dad. They could stay out and party all night. That escalated my life-style of staying out all night. I went to this school for about a year. I would be so stoned on quaaludes that I talked slow. When you do vallium and quaaludes, it slows your speech down to almost zero. The first hour of every day would be classroom book teaching on welding. There would be a classroom discussion and I couldn't even talk. Being high was like a drunk; the higher you got, the more you wanted to talk. You never realized you were drunk and you didn't realize how stupid you were acting. Everybody, including the instructor, (and there were twenty-four students in there) all knew I stayed stoned. They got high, too, but I was stoned. Every day whoever had money that day bought the beer.

We drank beer at lunch and smoked dope in the welding booths.

When the instructor would come by, we would go back to welding. I had a joint up under my welding shield a lot of times and would look right at the instructor. Of course he couldn't see the joint. I'd have it in my mouth, stand there, and nod my head at him with smoke coming out the top of my shield.

One afternoon, someone tapped me on the shoulder and said, "You have an urgent phone call. Your mother called and said you should call her back."

That morning I had sold a high school girl a hundred hits of speed. The first thing that hit me was so weird. I thought, "Oh man, that girl got busted, and she narced on me for selling her the speed."

I don't know what it was, but I had a feeling of dread and apprehension. I knew that something was wrong. I walked down the sidewalk, thirty yards to the pay phone, but it was like walking a mile. It seemed like it took me forever to get there. Everything that could possibly be wrong went through my head. Did my sister have a car wreck? Did I get busted for dope? Was the IRS at the house? What could be the problem? I dropped a dime in the phone and dialed the numbers. The phone rang and I dreaded the answer. I knew it wasn't your average call to the house to hear, "I want you to bring some milk home."

I knew something very bad was wrong. My mother answered the phone. I asked, "Mom, what is it now?"

She said, "Kelly, I don't know what we're going to do

this time; I can't help you!''

"What is it? What's wrong?'' I pleaded.

She said, "Moments ago there were two detectives at the house, and they had warrants for your arrest for the sale of drugs.''

Man, all kinds of emotions suddenly bombarded me. It was not that I was busted for drugs. I'd been busted before, but it was like now my mom knew. The world knew. Now I was an official drug pusher. That was a title I didn't like, I guess. Mom was sobbing. "Mom," I said, "Don't worry about it. I'll be right home. We'll take care of it. It's no big deal.''

She said, "Oh, yes, Kelly; it is a big deal.''

I went back into the classroom and started talking to all the guys. I said, "Hey, man they've just delivered warrants for my arrest.''

They were now trying to give me all this legal advice, like they knew and everything. I got out that afternoon at three o'clock. I was not concentrating on anything. When I got home, I called a lawyer we knew and he told me how to pre-arrange bail. I went down to the police station, and they booked me in and finger printed me. I was then out immediately on bail. The bail was thousands of dollars. We didn't have the money and had to put up my mother's house to bail me out. I was booked on three counts at the time.

I was out of jail, but I knew I was facing the penitentiary. I finally realized that I could go to jail. My charges were all felonies. I didn't know how many years a felony carried. I didn't know any of that. I knew I needed help and lots of it. I went to a prominent attorney in Montgomery. He was a big drug attorney who had defended every druggy in town there. He told me, "I'll take the case. It will cost you five thousand dollars per count on the drugs.

That is $15,000, and I can probably get you off with five years."

This guy was a big wig but he said, "You're going to jail."

I went to attorney after attorney after attorney. Everyone said the same thing: "Son, we can get you a reduced sentence, but you're going to the penitentiary. The best thing for you to do is save your money and get a court-appointed attorney. They're all good; we just take turns. One can do as good as the next on this case, but you're going to the penitentiary."

Everyone of them told me the same thing. So I went to my preliminary hearing. I asked the judge to give me a court-appointed attorney.

His name was Joe Dawkins. I think Joe was an atheist. I began telling my story and for some reason he liked me.

Instantly we related to each other and I could talk to him. I poured out everything. I mean everything. I told this guy things I had never shared with anyone. I talked about the drug world, about the system and the chain of command. I continued about the way the drugs were sold and some of the things that I had done which I thought nobody knew. God didn't even know about it. This underworld that I lived in was a totally real existing world but it co-existed with the "seen society" of America: we, the free enterprise system, the public school system, each part of the society as we see it. Then there's the underworld that at least three-fourths of the people don't even know about. It's a real existing, partying, drug-oriented, totally different world. It's real but it's invisible to most people. Joe had been a lawyer for fifteen years, and he couldn't believe some of the things that he was hearing. I was only nineteen years old and I said, "Man, I've been doing this since I was thirteen years old."

I told him about shooting the dope and the parties and all of it. After I told him all this stuff, after hours and hours, his synopsis was, "Kelly, you're in a very serious situation."

He really didn't know what else to say. Now meeting with him wasn't an hour today and an hour tomorrow and an hour the next day. This took several weeks. I met with him initially the day that he was appointed to me in the courtroom. He got all the information: my name, the cases, and of course, he gathered all the material from the district attorney and the court and everything that he needed so that he was aware of the legalities of my situation. This time I had gone too far.

9

MEETING GOD

I had a friend named Dewey who had been in prison for assault with intent to murder and for selling cocaine. Dewey accepted Christ in prison. I didn't even know the plan of salvation. I had been raised in church. I thought I was a Christian. I prayed every night. I even prayed after I got busted, "God help me."

I knew that I came from a good family. My grandparents were Methodists and my mom was Methodist, so I had the right to pray.

Dewey was a Lutheran. He had just gotten out of prison. God had gotten him out, but he didn't tell me that because I wouldn't have understood it. He had enough wisdom I guess to not scare me off and make me think he was crazy. There was something different about Dewey. He was a little short guy, about thirty, bald-headed, and he was always happy. He didn't have much money. He was a roofer and had to work like a dog.

He drove an old van, (and if I know him, he probably still has that stupid thing). Even after he started making money, he drove this van. I couldn't understand why

Dewey drove this stupid, old van. It didn't even have any paint on it, but he was always happy. I worked part-time with him sometimes. He'd hit his finger with a hammer and say, "Praise the Lord."

I thought, "This guy is an idiot."

My friend and I worked with Dewey off and on over a period of months. Dewey started inviting us to church. He'd say, "Hey, why don't you all come and go to church with me?"

Most of the guys laughed and joked about it. I defended church and would say, "Hey, man, you're wrong. You don't need to be laughing and cutting down church. You know God's real. I wouldn't laugh about God if I were you."

They would just laugh more and say, "Yea, Kelly, who are you to tell us about God?"

I would say, "Man, I'm a Christian and I believe there is a God. We will go to church with you one day, Dewey."

I can remember times when we'd be parked up on the Atlanta Highway ("the strip"), and these religious fanatics would come by passing out tracts. A lot of the kids tried to jump on them or start something. I would say, "Hey, you leave these guys alone."

I would stand there and listen to them and take the tracts.

I had so much respect for them that I would wait until they were out of eyesight before I threw the tracts away. I respected them. There was kind of a kindred spirit there with the Christians.

At the same time my oldest sister, Judy, had been married eight years and had two children. She and her husband started going to church again. They had met in the Methodist Church years before they had stopped going to church. My brother-in-law had just been discharged from the Air Force. They had moved back to Montgomery and were going to church with some cousins of mine I knew had never gone to church. All of a sudden all of these people who were around me were inviting me to church. I was on my way to prison. My response to my family was, "Get off my back, I don't need church. I don't need God. I'm going to prison. I've got my own set of problems. Talk to me about it later. Quit messing with my mind."

Every time I would see Judy, she would say, "Kelly, come to church with me, come to church with me, come to church with me."

Dewey was a little more subtle, but he kept saying, "Why don't you go to church with me this evening? Kelly, there is a guy preaching who you would really like. He really relates to young people. You would really love him. Why don't you..."

Finally to shut him up, we said, "OK, we'll go to church with you!"

There were six of us. We were all laughing. It wasn't a big deal and yet there was a fear of how I was going to act.

I hoped these guys wouldn't embarrass me when we got to church. I knew how to act. I had been to church many times.

Hey, these guys were rough. They were like a crew of sailors.

They were liable to cuss right in church. I didn't even own a suit, but Dewey said, "Don't worry about it. People wear jeans out there and everything."

Dewey let us go home early from roofing. We got all cleaned up and we were going to go to church. We met at Freddy's house. We all arrived early so we started drinking and gambling and by the time Dewey got there, we said, "Naw, we're not going, we're not going."

We didn't go! We even got off work early. Dewey was really disappointed and went on to church by himself.

The next day was Sunday and my sister Judy was over at the house. She was on me real strong. "Come on, Kelly, go to church with us tonight. Come on, you've been promising you would go."

I called my friends and said, "Man, my sister goes to the same church that Dewey goes to, and she says that this guy out there preaching is really great."

The only thing I knew about a revival was, as a little kid, a missionary from Africa brought these big masks, bones, and spears to church. I said, "It'll be all right, let's all go to church."

So all six of us got together that Sunday afternoon, got all dressed up, and then got high. Everyone wanted to back out again, but I said, "Naw, come on let's go this time." They finally agreed.

That Sunday night the preacher was Dwight Thompson. He preached on hell. We were sitting in the back cutting up. We were all high and drunk. We all felt conviction and God dealt with us, but we were so distracted by each other that it rolled off us like water off a duck. This was a Pentecostal Church.

I told the guys after church, "Man, there is no way that I will ever go back to that church again. That place is crazy."

God was wearing me out, but I didn't know it was God. I didn't think about anything but Hell all that night. Monday night some of the guys called, "Come on, man, let's shoot pool tonight."

I said, "Naw, I can't. I've got a date."

Of course I was lying. I called my sister and asked,

"Judy, is that revival still going?"

She said, "Yes."

I said, "Come by here and get me. I want to go with you."

When she picked me up, I said, "I sat in the balcony last night. Now I want to sit on the main floor, but I don't want to sit too close to the front."

We sat about halfway back. I can still see where I sat. It was at First Assembly of God in Montgomery. Dwight Thompson started preaching on heaven. That guy was one of the flashiest and best orators I had ever seen or heard. I had never seen a preacher like that. I had never even seen one like that on TV. He didn't get up there, stand behind the pulpit, and read his sermon. He was powerful and anointed! I was intrigued. I hadn't heard people talk about the flashy money preachers so I didn't have a bad concept of him. I was totally intrigued by him. It was like a show but really different. God was just wearing me out. (Now I'm not a genius or anything, but when a guy preaches on hell one night and heaven the next night, you don't have to be real smart to make a decision where you want to spend eternity.) When Dwight Thompson told a story, he told a story! He could talk about a tree house and you'd get scared of heights! I mean this guy could tell a story! He was telling about heaven. I started crying and he was only half-way through the message.

He was not even getting "hot and heavy" yet. I couldn't even remember the last time I had cried. I sat there telling myself, "Don't cry, don't cry, you're an idiot. There's a thousand people here looking at you, don't cry."

I sat there trying to hold my lips together as tight as I could and keep the tears in my eyes and not look stupid.

I was trying to keep my composure but thinking, "You're blowing it! Your sister is sitting here looking."

It was conviction. He was really preaching under God's anointing. The anointing was everywhere. Everybody else was shouting, "Amen," but I wasn't really aware of them around me.

Rev. Thompson's words came from the Bible:

"For the wages of sin is death..." (Romans 3:23)

"The wicked shall be turned into hell..." (Psalm 9:17)

"The saved shall dwell in the house of the Lord for ever..." (Psalm 23:6)

I could be sure of going to Heaven, "To an inheritance incorruptible, and undefiled, and that fadeth not away, reserved in heaven for you." (I Peter 1:4)

Those verses and his remarks were digging into my very gut.

I knew that Jesus Christ was my only hope! "God," I cried, "help me to have the strength to follow through on this. God, I need your help!"

I saw my sister looking at me out of the corner of her eye.

I turned the other way so she couldn't see my face. She knew what was happening, but I didn't. Finally the time came for the altar call. I wasn't going to play any games. I thought, "Man, this is it! I'm getting saved. I'm going to Heaven, not Hell!"

10

REV. COY BARKER

Somehow through the grapevine, Rev. Coy Barker, pastor of the First Assembly of God church, found out I was facing a prison sentence. I didn't know Coy Barker and had not even heard of him. One day out of the blue the phone rang and the voice on the other end said, "Kelly, this is Rev. Coy Barker. God told me today to call you."

I thought, "God spoke to you?"

He continued, "I want you to come out to my office. I want to talk to you because I think I can help you."

I just said, "OK." Then I thought, "This guy is crazy. He thinks God spoke to him."

I'd never heard anybody say that before. People in the Methodist Church never used that phrase. Pentecostals use that expression a lot, but I'd never heard anybody say God had spoken to them.

I told my mom, "I need to go out and see this guy face to face who is crazy enough to say that God spoke to him. I'd like to meet him and shake his hand just to see what kind of nut he really is."

So I went out to his office and was humbled! I stopped looking down my nose at him or thinking he was stupid. Coy Barker, who didn't know me, greeted me and said, "I want to help you, Kelly. Tell me your story."

All my friends had turned their backs on me. My drug buddies didn't want to come around me because they thought the police were watching me. Some family members wouldn't even help me. I asked my cousin, "You've known me all my life. You know how I was when I was in the drug world, but now I'm changed. I'm a Christian. I want you to be a character witness and tell the judge what a change you've seen in my life."

He flatly stated, "I won't help, Kelly; I've got no use for a drug pusher."

They turned their back on me once they found out I was a drug pusher. Brother, that was taboo. They wrote me off as if I didn't exist. My friends wouldn't help me. My family wouldn't help me. My neighbors wouldn't help me. Just my mother and sisters stood by me. That was it. Of course everybody's mothers and sisters, even if you were Charles Manson, would stand up and lie for you to keep you from going to prison. That had no credence to a judge or to a court.

However, Coy Barker wanted to hear my story. I sat in his office and told him about myself and the trouble I was in.

After hearing it all, he said, "Kelly, I want to go to court with you and be a character witness and tell them how God has changed your life."

I didn't really think that was going to have very much impact but didn't want to insult the man so I said, "OK, that's fine."

Coy's appearance and mannerisms were awesome. I had been around a lot of physically big people before but, there was something different about Coy Barker. I sensed it. When you met Coy Barker, you never forgot him. Nobody ever dismissed Coy Barker. He was not an overbearing, domineering kind of person, even in a casual meeting. But if you met him in a mall, you would take a look and not forget him. I went home flying on cloud nine. I told my mom, "That preacher, Coy Barker, wants to go to court with me." Mom got all excited.

I met with my lawyer again and said, "Joe, I got saved at church a couple of days ago."

He exclaimed, "You did! That's great; that will be something we can use in court."

I said, "Yeah, and my preacher called me and wants to testify as a character witness."

My lawyer had said to get myself four or five good character witnesses. Heaven knew I had been trying. Joe continued, "He does? He wants to be a character witness? That's good."

I said, "Yes, he's going to come and tell the judge that I got saved and that he was there and saw it and everything. He will also swear that I am now a different person and that I am not going to do drugs anymore. He'll tell the court that it doesn't have to worry about me again."

The lawyer laughed and said, "Kelly, everybody that gets busted and arrested for anything has a religious conversion and tries to get a preacher to come and testify. Everybody does that. Don't get your hopes up. That's not going to help. It's going to look good but everybody does it. It's just understood that you make a good effort when you go to court and if you can get a preacher to go and testify for you it always helps. But, Kelly, again I warn you; don't get your hopes up."

I asked, "Listen, Joe, what's our plan of defense? What are we going to do when we go to court?"

He explained, "What we need to do is try to get the judge to drop as many counts as he will or at least say that he will run the sentences concurrently. However, Kelly, I've got bad news for you. You drew Judge Sam Taylor as your judge.

"They call him "Stern Sam". It seems like the circumstances and luck are stacked against us. There's not a worse draw you could have gotten on a judge than him. On drug or sex-related crimes, he throws the book at the offender."

Joe really started to "build me up and encourage" as he continued, "Not long ago there was a kid that went in front of Judge Taylor for a crime that was drug related, not even selling. It was like one count of possession with intent to sell. He gave him eight years in the penitentiary."

I couldn't believe what I was hearing. I was scared to death, but I said, "Listen, Joe; here's what I think we should do. New Christians have a lot of zeal and a lot of blind faith, I guess, but I want us to plead guilty and then ask for probation."

Joe just laughed and said, "You're crazy, man! You have three felony charges. That's potentially forty-five years. You can't ask for probation. That's a slap on the hand.

"You've been busted. You've got a record a mile long for possession, arrests for DWI's for fights, for assaults, for criminal trespasses. Your record as a juvenile is a mile long. You are now nineteen. I have already beed to court and asked for Y. O. A. status (youth offenders act) so they would try you as a juvenile, and they have denied that. You're being tried as an adult in the state of Alabama.

They're going to send you to the penitentiary. There is no way around it. I have personally seen literally dozens of cases just like this. Kelly, you have had it! There is no way that you can ask for probation. The thing to do is to plea bargain with the court. Plead guilty and throw yourself on the mercy of the court. Tell them that you will turn in some other pushers. You can turn state's evidence and ask them to reduce your sentence. I can get you off with just five years. Take what you can get. If you go in there with no defense, don't plea bargain, don't offer them anything; they're going to give you fifteen years in the penitentiary. That's the bottom line."

Joe thought he had convinced me because the next time I came to visit him, he started telling me that he had made a deal with the D.A. so that he would drop this and that count if I turned in this person or that person. I said, "Look, I am pleading guilty and I am asking for probation. I am not turning anybody in and I am not asking for anything. We're pleading guilty and I'm asking for probation. God told me that."

That was the first time I'd ever said those words. I thought that if it would work for Coy Barker, it would work for me. I just knew I didn't have to go to the penitentiary.

I felt like God had said to me that He didn't save me so I would spend my life in jail. He saved me so that I could help other people. Joe gave me a very strange and puzzled look and replied, "Kelly, as your attorney, I am strictly advising you that is the wrong thing to do, but I am bound by your desire, and I have to do what you want. I should back out of the case and take myself off it because you're going to make us both look stupid. You're going to go to prison, for God only knows how long, and I'm going to look dumb. But I won't quit; for some reason I'm going to go through with this. I know I'm stupid, but I'll stick with you.''

The following Wednesday we had to go to court. We decided we were going to plead guilty and were going to ask for probation. Joe still said it wouldn't work and gave me zero hope. On Tuesday Joe met with my whole family and me and said, "Kelly is going to the penitentiary. There is no way around it. He's going to the penitentiary.''

I was charged with selling marijuana, cocaine, and quaaludes. I had sold these to narcotic agents over a period of a year eight different times and they had witnesses. They had me dead to rights. There was no way that I could go in there and say I had not sold the drugs or that it was a mistaken identity. We were going the next day (Wednesday) to my pre-sentence hearing. I was then going to be sentenced on Friday. I was still out on bond.

I had always prided myself and made the statement often, "I can smell a narc a mile away. I'll never get busted. I can smell those pigs a mile off." Before the hearing, however, I began remembering the complete incident with Rene.

Rene, the girl I had gotten busted with back in the twelfth grade, had been arrested and taken downtown for holding out on the quaaludes. Unknown to me, the police made a deal with her. They let her off by getting her to promise to set me up.

I had forgotten all about Rene. I didn't even remember her name. She called me one day and said, "Hey, Kelly, my boy friend and I are going to the river skiing and we need some coke.''

I said, "OK, I'll meet you up at Godon's Meat Market.''

I used that parking lot many times to sell drugs. The market was at a small shopping center. I met them there about an hour later and sold them some cocaine. Her boy friend had a yankee accent and was dressed in blue jeans. He called me several times after that, and I sold him some quaaludes and marijuana. He even came to my house and I sold him dope.

Sometimes when I met him, he would be dressed in greasy blue jeans and a blue jean vest with oil on it. He often smelled like gas so I thought he was a mechanic. I sold him a lot of drugs over a period of a year.

For some reason, the last time I was to sell to him I suspected he was a narc. I called my friend Jim and said, "Jim, I want you to go with me and drive my car. I am going to meet this guy and sell him some drugs tonight."

He had made a mistake and I just knew he was a narc. Jim had just gotten a Monte Carlo. He had bought it used, and it had a plate on the front which read "Cliff." My pusher, Benny, lived in a big, ritzy neighborhood, and a detective had found out who he was and where he lived. The police rented a vacant house across the street from Benny for surveillance. The day before, Jim and I drove up to my pusher's house and parked the car in front. We went in, got our drugs, came back out, and left. The next day, Rene's boy friend called me and said, "Hey, I drove by Benny's house and saw you and Cliff over there."

Right then, I thought, "I don't know anybody named Cliff. That was Jim's car." He had seen the "Cliff" name plate on the front of it and tried to make quick conversation.

I made the connection in my mind, and it hit me, "That guy's a narc. He doesn't know Cliff from Jim. He was trying to be cool and pop these names off and act like he knows the circle of people that I know. He is a narc, and I have been selling him dope for a year."

I told Jim all about the guy and said, "I'm meeting him tonight, and I'm going to have to deal with him because he's a narc."

So Jim picked me up. I got into the back seat, and we drove to the Wynn-Dixie parking lot off the Atlanta Highway. We pulled into the parking lot and stopped. Immediately this guy pulled up, and another guy started to come over to the car. I called, "Hey, come on and get in the car, but tell your partner to stay in the car."

To me that was simply a figure of speech, like tell your "friend" to stay in the car. He stopped and I saw fear flash across his face for a split second. I thought, "Oh, no, I said 'partner'."

So he told him, "Stay in the car."

He realized that I knew, and he didn't want to get in the car. He most likely knew I had a gun in the car and thought if he turned around and started off, I would shoot him. I don't know if I would have or not. He got in the car and brother was he nervous. I mean he was NERVOUS. I was sitting there in the back seat and we drove off. I said, "Hello, Officer Danny. You've been pretty slick, haven't you?"

"What are you talking about? You're talking crazy, Turner. What's your problem?" he asked.

He was still trying to maintain his cover. He didn't know if I was going to kill him or what. Then I said, "Brother, I know you're a narc and I should kill you."

All of a sudden he busted out, "Everybody in town knows I'm with you! Every cop in town knows I'm with you. If you kill me..."

I said, "I'm not going to kill you. I know you're a narc so I'm not selling any more drugs to you. You're probably going to get me busted, but I'll get you if you do. I'll get you.''

We then drove back to the store and dropped him off. Three months went by and nothing happened. I told Jim, "I was an idiot. That guy wasn't a narc. He hasn't called me back because he thinks I'm crazy. He thought I was going to kill him. I accused a guy of being a narc and he wasn't.''

I realized he was. The police had not only tried to set me up; they wanted connections off me. It had taken the grand jury that long to put the indictments together. The State had an open-and-shut, hard-clad case.

The dreaded Wednesday morning finally arrived. Coy Barker came by my house and picked up my mother and me. My sisters followed us in their car. We went first to my attorney's office, which was right across the street from the courthouse. Joe Dawkins, my attorney, talked with us and again told us how serious the situation was.

He said, "This is most likely what is going to happen this morning. We'll go to the courtroom and there are probably several cases in front of you. This is a pre-sentence hearing. The purpose of this hearing is for you to present to the judge any reason why he should sentence you lightly because you have pleaded guilty. He'll say, 'State of Alabama versus Kelly Turner, case No. so and so.' He'll ask me to stand as the lawyer and you, Kelly, to stand as the defendant. He'll read the charges, and then he'll ask us if we have anything to say. Then, Kelly, you can be seated and I'll present Rev. Barker.''

As he spoke, I could hardly breathe. Suddenly, I realized I was in serious trouble. As we walked across the street, I felt like a sheep being led to the slaughterhouse. I thought my knees would buckle as I walked.

Slowly, we walked into the courtroom. We were told

to be seated. I sat there, too dazed and afraid to look around. I prayed, "God, I hope I really heard you. Pastor Barker really thinks You are going to do something for me. God, my lawyer has told me time and time again that I will be sentenced and go to the State Penitentiary. God I am afraid. Please help me. I don't deserve it, but I'm pleading with You."

Suddenly I heard the judge say, "State of Alabama versus Kelly Turner, Case Number 8666."

Joe shook me and said, "Kelly, stand up!"

My poor mother was sitting there trembling, with tears streaming down her cheeks. What a creep I was for putting her through this living hell. My sisters sat there, also, not knowing what to do.

After the preliminaries were over, the judge said to my lawyer, "Mr. Dawkins, what do you have to say in Kelly Turner's defense?"

The attorney said, "Your Honor, Kelly would like to speak to the court."

I caught my breath, prayed, then spoke: "Your Honor, God has saved me. I realize what I did was wrong. I'm guilty. I don't deny it and I'm not going to lie about it. I've sold dope and I've taken dope all of my teenage life. I've been caught and I know it was wrong. But Jesus has saved me and the only thing that I have to say is if I am let off, I won't do it again. That is all I can say."

I sat down and prayed.

The lawyer spoke again, "Your Honor, we have one character witness: his pastor, Rev. Coy Barker."

Rev. Coy Barker walked out from behind the table and stood right up in front of the judge's bench. He was almost eyeball to eyeball with the judge. Rev. Barker stared at the judge for a moment and then said, "Your

Honor, we're not asking for justice; we're asking for mercy."

He turned around and he started to walk away from the bench and I thought, "Big Whoopie! This guy comes down here and tells me he's going to help me and that's all he says?"

Then Rev. Barker wheeled back around and pointed his finger at the judge and laid his other hand on the judge's big desk.

He had his finger about a foot from the judge's face when he said, "Your Honor, God says, 'You won't sleep till you've made the right decision to let this boy off.' "

He then turned around and walked off.

I thought, "Dear God, he has just buried me. Why did he stick his finger in the judge's face?"

My attorney looked at me in total anguish and bewilderment.

I could hardly catch my breath as I whispered, "Joe, I didn't ask him to come down here. He told me he was coming. What are we going to do?"

The judge almost barked, "Is there anyone else who has anything to say?"

I mean he was miffed. My attorney responded, "No, your Honor, there is no one else, thank you."

The judge got up, gathered his papers, wrapped his robe around him, and stomped out. He was mad. He was upset. This big smart-aleck preacher pointed his finger in his face and told him the judgement of God was coming down on him, and he was not going to sleep. My only witness turned out to be like the last nail in my coffin. Rev. Coy Barker had blown my chances! I was headed for jail!

Rev. Coy Barker

11

NOT JUSTICE,
BUT MERCY

After Rev. Coy Barker's escapade with the judge, I went home totally defeated, full of anxiety and fear. I could hardly talk to anyone. All I could hear were the words of my lawyer ringing in my ears, "Kelly, you are going to the penitentiary. Kelly, you are going to the penitentiary, penitentiary, penitentiary."

I thought I would go crazy.

I knew the lawyer was only trying to prepare me for the worst. But I was scared spitless.

The last thing he told me before he walked out of the courtroom was, "Kelly, Friday bring a change of underclothes and your overnight case with your razor, toothbrush, and everything because they'll be taking you upstairs after sentencing. Once they sentence you, they won't let you go home and get anything. They will take you straight up to the jail."

That was his confidence and contingency over the months. He never wavered: "You are going to the penitentiary."

From a legal standpoint he knew there was no way

out. I was trying to believe God had spoken to me, but the expert knew there was no way out! He had told me of all kinds of lesser crimes where people got very long sentences. It was his deepest desire to instill in me the fact that there was no hope so that I wouldn't build up any false hopes. He had done his job well, for all my hope was gone.

Montgomery's First Assembly of God had its prayer meeting and Bible Study on Thursday night. We all went to church.

Down deep, I knew if I had any hope at all, it was with God! My thoughts and feelings were confused.

The church members knew all about my problems and had really been praying for me. At times my faith had been that of a giant. But after Coy Barker's words to the judge, I wasn't so sure.

I was trying to be real cool and act like I had all the faith in the world. But when Coy Barker walked into the church, I almost lost it. I didn't realize he could be a real prophet of God.

Coy went to the pulpit and said, "Will Mrs. Turner and Kelly please come to the front."

Slowly we walked up to the front of the church. Coy put his hand on my shoulder and asked, "Kelly, do you believe God said that you would not go to jail?"

In sheer faith I said, "Yes."

Then he turned to the congregation and said, "I believe it is the will of God that Kelly Turner be set free. Yesterday in court, I told the judge God would not let him sleep until he made the right decision. Now I want us to pray that God will keep that man awake. I know as I speak that he has not reached a decision concerning Kelly. Stand and stretch forth your hands toward Kelly."

As those hundreds of hands stretched forth, I could sense the very presence of the Holy Spirit. Coy Barker prayed a prayer of faith like I had never heard. He was without a doubt, standing in the very Throne Room of God.

After the service, everyone was telling me that I would be delivered. I went home full of faith and hope.

"Mom, I really believe God is going to do a miracle for me. Everything will be all right. I'll see you in the morning."

I went to my room, undressed, and got ready for bed. I knelt by my bed and prayed, giving thanks for God's promises.

I turned out the light and climbed into bed.

Suddenly, fear hit me! I was attacked by a barrage of satanic spirits. All hell broke loose on me. My mind was under attack.

I had been to jail before — having been arrested for assault, trespassing, drunk driving, and possession of dope.

I was being tormented thinking about the reality of going to prison. My lawyer had told me I was going to prison and there was no way around it. He gave me the encouragement that I could possibly get off with just five years.

I began thinking of the different times I'd been to jail.

One time in particular came to mind — when I was in Lee County Jail. John and I were at a state park there. It was off-season and we climbed over a locked fence, took one of the boats off the dock, and went riding around. We stopped the boat in the middle of the lake and were sitting there smoking dope and getting high. We then heard someone over a bull horn, telling us to come to shore. We took the boat to shore and were arrested by the county sheriff and taken to the Lee County Jail. The jail was infamous for overcrowding, riots, rapes, and everything else that prisons are noted for.

I was eighteen at the time. They put me in a place called the Bull Hole, which years ago used to be the drunk tank. Because the jail was so overcrowded, it was used as a holding tank.

It was on the third floor. Being an interior cell, there were no exterior windows. It was about two o'clock in the afternoon and all the power went out. It was totally, one-hundred-percent pitch black. You could not see your hand in front of your face. The prisoners began to set paper on fire and throw it out on the catwalk in an effort to cause confusion. The smoke was so intense you couldn't breathe and had to get low to the ground to get any air. That went on for several hours. The power was off so all the vent fans were out and was it hot! It was in the middle of summer and at least 110 degrees in there.

I felt an arm grip my shoulder and it held me tight.

Someone began speaking in a low voice: "I'm in here for twenty-eight years for rape, and kid, you are going to be my woman."

He went on to tell me in detail all the things that would happen to me if I didn't do what he said. I never even responded to him. I just sat there in dead silence. The lights came on and I wondered who had spoken to me. What was I going to do?

Thank God soon after, someone posted bail and I was free to go. I had to go back to see the judge for sentencing for stealing this boat and trespassing on state property. The judge was infuriated that the sheriff's deputies had even put me, an eighteen-year-old, in that Bull Hole for such a small offense. He told my mother and me the story of the kid who had been there one week before me.

He was also eighteen years old, and the prisoners had tried to rape him, but he would not give in. They began to beat and kick him in the head. One of them kicked him so hard that his eyeball popped out of the socket. One of the other prisoners walked over and stepped on it and squashed it. Then they went on and raped him.

All of these kinds of thoughts were going through my mind.

I was in torment and didn't sleep one moment all night. The voices seemed to scream at me, "Kelly, you're next. They will rape and beat you. You don't stand a chance. You will see then what kind of a God you have."

"Kelly! Kelly, it's time to get up and get ready for court. Breakfast will be ready in fifteen minutes." I heard Mom shout as I rolled out of bed.

Satan had really done a number all night long on my mind.

When my mom, three sisters, and I got into the car to go to the lawyer's office it was like we were going to a funeral and it would be mine.

My lawyer was laying ninety-nine-to-one odds that I was going to prison. We drove to the lawyer's office without my overnight case. I kind of did that as an act of faith. I intentionally did not take anything because I didn't plan to stay — although I was unsure. It was faith in operation. I wanted to show God in my feeble way that I believed Him. We once again walked across the street to the courthouse. The lawyer sat us down.

Joe spoke to Mom in a real tender but stern voice: "Mrs. Turner, I really have come to respect and like Kelly very much. I am certain he is a changed boy. However, he doesn't seem to realize that in a few moments he is going to be sentenced and sent to the State Penitentiary.

I told him to bring his personal belongings and he didn't. They will not let him go anywhere after he is sentenced. So if you will go back to your house and bring me his things, after this is over, I will see that they are taken to him. I am sorry to be so blunt, but I don't want you to get hurt any more than necessary with false hopes."

Coy Barker was not in the courtroom. When he prayed the night before, he fully believed I would not be going to jail.

I would be free to come by the church and see him. How I hoped and prayed that his faith was real, because he had it!

Then the bailiff spoke: "Please rise. The County Court is now in session; the Honorable Judge Samuel Taylor presiding."

The judge entered and we were seated. Judge Taylor said, "Case number 8666, that of Kelly Turner, is now before this bench. Mr. Turner, please stand."

I sat there almost unable to move. My knees were like putty. Slowly I rose to my feet. The judge continued, "Mr. Turner, before I pass sentence, do you have anything you would like to say?"

"No, your Honor, I have nothing to say."

That is what my lawyer told me to say. I thought to myself, "What did he mean when he said, 'Before I sentence you'?"

Without emotion the judge spoke again: "Mr. Turner, therefore, this court finds you guilty of three counts of selling and delivering drugs. The State of Alabama sentences you to five years in the State Penitentiary!"

He then deliberately closed his folder.

I felt like a mule had kicked me in my stomach. I stood there dazed. "God," I said, "You have forsaken me and let me down. You have made a fool of me. I have been witnessing about Jesus and telling everybody that You are for real and that You even told me that I would be free. You let me down."

My mother was crying and I was helpless. It was like I had been sentenced to death.

I think I was near fainting when the judge slowly raised his head, looked directly into my eyes, and said, "Mr. Turner, after much thought and deliberation on my part, this court is going to suspend that sentence and give you five years probation. If, however, you break your probation, you will then serve your sentence of five years in the State Penitentiary."

He then turned and walked out of the courtroom. I was too stunned for a moment to say or do anything but weep. "Jesus, forgive me for not completely trusting You," I prayed.

My lawyer just freaked. He looked at me and said, "Five years probation! Nobody gets five years probation. He could have given you a year in the penitentiary and a year of probation but five years probation?"

I wanted out of that courtroom and right then! We went into the hall and had church. My lawyer was still stunned. He was in total, one-hundred-percent, complete disbelief. He came out into the hall and began jumping up and down with us. He couldn't believe it and even he got carried away. "Man, I've never seen anything like it! That was Stern Sam. Kelly, you did get a miracle."

I was out there hollering, "Praise God. Thank you, Jesus. Thank you, Jesus."

As we left the courthouse I said, "Joe, thanks. I appreciate your help. God bless you, man."

He was an atheist as far as I know, but he was great

and we'd become good friends. He had even told me stuff about himself. It had been like we were each other's counselors and had been real close.

On the way home, it hit me. Coy Barker was really a prophet of God. He did hear God speak and spoke without fear of what God had said to him. WOW! God was really for real.

The first thing I did was call Coy Barker. When he answered the phone, I cried, "Brother Barker, I'm free! Jesus set me free! Man, you were right on. Jesus did it. He set me free! God changed Judge Taylor's mind. Do you hear me? I'm free!"

On Sunday we went to church and there was a barrage of people all around us saying, "We knew God would come through. Praise the Lord!"

The church had two Sunday morning services because of the crowds. At the beginning of the second service, I was somewhat nervous because of all the attention. I looked around and there stood Sam Taylor, the judge; Jimmy Evans, the district attorney; and Joe Dawkins, my lawyer. I thought, "Oh God, what are they doing here?"

Fear hit me and I sank in my seat. That wasn't reasonable thinking but...after church I didn't go running up to them to shake their hands or anything. I really didn't want them to see me. I saw them talking to Rev. Barker and he was crying.

As soon as they left, I went to Rev. Barker to find out what had happened. The judge had come back to God. The district attorney, who had once attended our church, also had come back to God and my lawyer had accepted Christ and had become a Christian!

The judge had told Rev. Barker, "God told me not to send that boy to the penitentiary. The night before the sentencing, I didn't even think about Kelly Turner, but I couldn't sleep. I had decided that morning to give him five years. However, when I closed the folder, something spoke to me, 'You are sleepy right now. You are going to be like this for a long time if you send this boy to the penitentiary because you have made a wrong decision.' That's when I looked back up and said, 'I suspend this sentence.' "

The words of Coy Barker suddenly rang in my ears, "Judge, we are not asking for justice, but mercy."

Joe Dawkins II

Kelly with his mother and sisters

Kelly and wife Laurie

12

GOD LOVES ME

Soon after I found Christ as my Savior, I started getting invitations to give my testimony to various churches and youth groups. Man, I was on my way. I was living high on Jesus. Nothing or no one could stop me now! I stopped cussing. I mean I had a filthy mouth! I couldn't say five words to anybody without cussing. My desire for drugs left me. I didn't do any more drugs. I was free! The need for alcohol left. I didn't drink anymore. However, I still smoked cigarettes for a long time. I was instantly "Mr. Clean" and had a hard time with those who weren't. I had seen a lot of people become Christians, get in, and then backslide with nobody trying to restore them. And they are still out.

One morning I woke up so full of condemnation I began wondering if I could make it through the day and remain a Christian. "How many years can I go on being a Christian?" I asked myself. That question always seemed to be on my mind.

Every day was a battle to be a Christian and to say, "I'm saved by the power of the Holy Ghost." I had to struggle not to do what was bad.

There was still a temptation to get high, a temptation to get drunk, a temptation for sex, and there was a temptation to go to movies I shouldn't go to. I still had a temper and I still had many problems. I would hear people testify, "There is nothing I like better than to read God's Word; I can just sit down and read God's Word for hours, and it jumps off the page at me." Or "The most precious times of my life are when I'm down on my knees in prayer before God."

It was hard for me to sit down and spend ten minutes in the Word. It was just as impossible for me to pray for an hour or to fast for days. I was trying to live as close to God as I knew how. While I was in church I felt like I could conquer the world. However, when I would get out of church and go back to work and school, everyday real life was a battle. I simply, by gut force, endured. The things the preacher said I had to do to be a good Christian were laborious to me. It was work — something I had to force myself to do. It was not spontaneous, or something that just happened. I had to force myself to stay away from wrong associations. I had to read my Bible even though I didn't always enjoy reading it. I had to pray even though I didn't always enjoy doing it.

Then one day my best friend, John, called. He was the one I had done everything with. We'd fought together, chased women together, got drunktogether, got high together — you name it and we did it together. When I answered the phone he asked, "Kelly, it has been a long time. I would like to come over and see you."

"Sure, come on over," I replied.

I totally walked away from all my doper friends, almost one hundred percent. Most of them didn't want anything to do with me anyway because I wasn't doing their thing, and the rest of them thought I was marked because I'd been busted. They thought I was still being watched. I got off so easily that a lot of them thought I had turned state's evidence. They didn't know or understand that God had gotten me off. They thought I had made a deal with the police. I still had some communication with John. John came right over to my house after he called. It was a Thursday afternoon.

"Kelly, it is my birthday today. Why don't you come out to the speakeasy tonight?" he asked. "I'm throwing a birthday party."

I said, "I can't come out there, man. I'm a Christian. I don't hang out at places like that anymore."

It was a big bar and disco. The disco was really the "in thing" and I really loved to dance. "Come on, Kelly, just come out there. You don't have to drink or nothing. Just come out there and be with us. It's my birthday," he argued.

I said, "All right I'll drop by after church."

So I went to church and then went to the speakeasy. I went right up to John's table, as he was the guest of honor, and sat down. "Well, Kelly, let me buy you a drink," John said.

"No, I don't want one," I responded, and I ordered a 7UP.

"Let me get you a drink," John demanded in a mad tone of voice. "You're not going to drink even one drink with me to celebrate my birthday? What kind of a friend and Christian are you?"

So I said, "OK, John, but just buy me one drink."

Of course as soon as I took the first sip that was it! Condemnation came on me everywhere. I had committed the "unpardonable sin" when I took a sip of alcohol. I thought, "Man, now I've sinned. I've let God down and I promised God I wouldn't do this and now I've done it. I'm going to hell so I might as well forget trying to be a Christian. There is no repentance so I might as well get smashed."

I can hardly remember what happened or how I got home. When I got up the next morning, I felt terrible. I really had a hangover and a pounding headache. But more seriously than that, I felt alone and empty.

"Jesus has left me," I thought. "I'm going to hell. It is impossible to live the Christian life. What's the use? I want to live the Christian life, I have really tried, bit I simply can't do it! I won't tell Mom or Coy Barker. I can't hurt them after all the trouble I have caused. I will continue to go to church and play the part of a Christian. I will just have to lead two lives."

I soon was on satan's merry-go-round. Dope, booze, sex — booze, sex, dope. The wheel turned faster and faster. I was on a collision course with death and no one knew.

While John and I were drinking, he asked me, "Kelly, why did you go through all the church and religion and God thing?"

I knew what I was going to say, and it was like the last straw that broke the camel's back. I knew then there was no turning back to God. I said, "John, you'd do anything when you're going to prison."

I didn't mean that. As soon as I said it, I knew I didn't mean it. I felt such condemnation when I said that about God that I knew there was no turning back. I wasn't going to get back to God.

Everyone at church thought I was an angel. I was, but a fallen one with no hope. I had been deceived and didn't know it. If I had only known Psalm 89:33: "My loving kindness will I not utterly take from him, nor suffer my faithfulness to fail." Or Romans 5:8: "God commendeth His love toward us, in that, while we were yet sinners, Christ died for us." Or Ephesians 2:45: "God who is rich in mercy, for His great love wherewith He loved us, even when we were dead in sins, hath quickened us together with Christ." Or I John 1:9: "If we confess our sins He is faithful and just to forgive us our sins, and to cleanse us from all unrighteousness."

As a result I let go. This insane nightmare continued for about three weeks. This happened in the middle of summer. One Friday night I went out and really tied one on. Again I don't remember getting into bed but remember the heat and humidity.

The sun came in the window and woke me. I lay there in my bed at ten o'clock on Saturday morning. My windows were open.

It was hot, and I had a pounding, rip-roaring hang over. I was sweating and just feeling plain miserable. Then I heard the doorbell ring and thought, "Oh, God, who is that?"

I heard my mother go to the door. I heard her say, "Yes, he is. Come in, Mr. Sorensen. I will get him."

"Oh no, its Sonny Sorensen. He moves in the gifts of the Spirit. He is weird."

My sister knew Sonny, but I had never met the man before. I would see him at church. He was a big guy. He didn't have a job, to my knowledge, but lived in a nice apartment. He drove a big car and always had on jewelry. The last person I wanted to see was one of those idiots from church — even though I had been going to church, keeping up appearances. I sat there and "Amened" like everyone else. I had to. I was responsible to Coy Barker for he had helped get me out of prison.

(There's nothing meaner than a backsliden Pentecostal...nothing meaner! You think you're going to hell, so what do you care about anybody else?) My momma knocked on the door and came in to my bedroom and announced, "There's somebody here to see you. It's Sonny Sorensen from church."

I said, "Tell him I'm not here."

She said, "I have already told him you are and he's sitting in the kitchen at the table waiting on you."

"I'm not seeing him. I don't care if he is. I'm not seeing him."

"Kelly, please, for my sake."

Now mom knew what was going on, but I hadn't told her.

(People aren't blind like we think they are.) I went to the kitchen. I didn't have on anything but jeans; no shirt, no shoes. I was smoking a cigarette and my hair was all messed up. I must have looked like death warmed over, and to top it off, I had a headache. I sat down at the table and looked at him with my best poker face. I was not giving away anything.

I asked, "What do you want?"

He said, "God sent me here."

"Is that right?" I said with all the sarcasm I could muster.

I was calloused. I wasn't going to take any of this Christian crap. "What did God send you over here for?"

"God told me twenty-one things and I wrote them down. Kelly, God wants me to share them with you."

I said, "I doubt that, but, all right, shoot."

I sat there and stared at him. I knew hate was radiating out of me. (Sonny told me later that he didn't know if I was going to kill him or what.) He was right with God and I wasn't. There was enmity between us. I hated him. He then started, "God says that you have rebellion in your heart toward authority because of the way that you were raised. You had rebellion in your heart against your dad, against all authority. That's why you can't submit to a pastor. That is also why you always have to dominate in dating relationships. That's why you always have to be the boss in your friendships."

He continued on down the list telling me this personal stuff that I had never related. It was all true, but I didn't want to hear it. I didn't want to admit it. He told me several other things, and then he said, "God told me that He's not mad at you because you told your friend that you'd do anything when you're going to prison."

It infuriated me that he knew I had said that. I stood and slammed my fist on the table. I looked at him and said, "You've got five minutes to finish what you've got to say, and then I want you to get out."

He said, "God told me to tell you to beware of Walter."

I said, "Friend, I don't even know anybody named Walter."

About the time I told him he had five minutes to finish, we heard the mail box flap hit, and my mother got the mail. She brought me some mail, and the return address on the envelope was The Walter Hoving Foundation. I wasn't about to let him see that. I thought, "No."

I opened it up, and it was a letter from a girl I had been dating who was a practicing witch. I had even dated her while I was saved. Man, when I opened that, I almost passed out.

God had already dealt with me about not seeing this girl anymore. Now because of drugs and rebellion, she was at this Walter Hoving Foundation home. God had sent that prophet there to tell me not to date or to see this girl anymore.

That was it! Right then and there! I gave in. I threw the letter at Sonny and said, "You might as well see this; you'll know it sooner or later. You know you're right on."

God sent a prophet to my house to get me back into the sheepfold. That showed me God was not mad at me. It didn't matter how many people He had to send to me or what kind of supernatural things had to occur. He had to for He loved me! (God will do whatever it takes to bring you back. It doesn't take as much for some people, and it takes more for others like me. Jesus will leave the ninety-nine to go back and get the one. He'll do anything.)

That's the fallacy in the Church today: If you aren't perfect, God can't use you and God is mad at you. I don't think God gets mad at His people, at least not in the sense of wrath. If you have sex, God doesn't say, "I'll destroy you or I'll never use you again."

(The thing that makes God the happiest is when we listen to the Holy Spirit and allow any conviction to have its effect on our lives. We can get back in a right relationship with God and with each other.)

What's going to happen to all these poor teenagers out there? They're going to sin; then they're going to get into condemnation and quit coming to church because they are ashamed.

The first thing I noticed happening in my life when I got in that situation was I became ashamed to go back to church.

I thought everybody knew what I'd been up to. I thought everybody could look at me and could tell I had not been living up to the things I had been preaching. But even if they had known and watched with their very own eyes, their position to me should have been to love me and restore me.

We should say, "Hey, man, you made a mistake. It's not the end of the world. Let's get back in this thing and get you restored and get you back into the Kingdom, in the service of Jesus."

"Kelly, before I go, I want to pray with you." Sonny began, "I want you to give your life back to God, and I know you will. However, now is the time God wants to deliver you from cigarettes."

I thought for a moment how I really loved Jesus and His church. I knew I had victory over the booze, drugs, cussing and sex, but cigarettes was a different matter. I was physically addicted to them. I would attend the first service at church and have to rush to my car for a quick cigarette before I could attend the second service. I wanted to be free, and I knew this was my moment.

"Sonny, I really thank you for obeying God and coming to see me," I cried.

With tears running down my cheeks, I asked him to pray.

Sonny laid his hands on my head and began to pray, "Dear God, I come to you in the name of Jesus Christ, Your Son. I ask in Jesus' name, God, that You deliver Kelly Turner from cigarettes. Never let him have the desire for nicotine again. In Jesus' name, Amen."

"Before you go, Sonny," I asked, "I would like to pray."

Now I began, "Lord, I really goofed up. Thank you for sending Sonny to speak to me. I know now that You love me and I accept Your promise that You will never leave me or forsake me. Thank you for Your forgiveness and love. Amen."

Sonny left and Mom cried and cried. Her son was back in the fold.

How I marvel at the mercy of God. He loved me so much that He sent His Son Jesus to die for me. I couldn't have cared less, but He did it anyway.

What God has done for me, He will do for YOU. His mercy and love is for everyone. Jesus Christ loves you and desires to forgive you.

David wrote it so well in Psalm 25:3-10: "None who have faith in God will ever be disgraced for trusting him. But all who harm the innocent shall be defeated. Show me the path where I should go, O Lord; point out the right road for me to walk. Lead me; teach me; for you are the God who gives me salvation. I have no hope except in you. Overlook my youthful sins, O Lord! Look at me instead through eyes of mercy and forgiveness, through eyes of everlasting love and kindness.

The Lord is good and glad to teach the proper path to all who go astray; He will teach the ways that are right and best to those who humbly turn to him. And when we obey him, every path he guides us on is fragrant with his loving kindness and his truth."

Truly in my life I was given mercy, not justice.

THE END